HUMAN MORALITY

HUMAN MORALITY

SAMUEL SCHEFFLER

OXFORD UNIVERSITY PRESS
New York   Oxford

Oxford University Press

Oxford   New York   Toronto
Delhi   Bombay   Calcutta   Madras   Karachi
Kuala Lumpur   Singapore   Hong Kong   Tokyo
Nairobi   Dar es Salaam   Cape Town
Melbourne   Auckland   Madrid

and associated companies in
Berlin   Ibadan

First published in 1992 by Oxford University Press, Inc.,
200 Madison Avenue, New York, New York 10016

First issued as an Oxford University Press paperback, 1993

Oxford is a registered trademark of Oxford University Press, Inc.

Library of Congress Cataloging-in-Publication Data
Scheffler, Samuel, 1951–
Human morality / Samuel Scheffler.
p.   cm. — Includes index.
ISBN 0-19-507448-3
ISBN 0-19-508564-7 (pbk.)
1. Ethics.   I. Title
BJ1012.S34   1992   170—dc20   91-35625

2   4   6   8   9   7   5   3   1

Printed in the United States of America
on acid-free paper

For Katy

ACKNOWLEDGMENTS

Much of the work on this book was done during two sabbatical leaves, one in 1984–85 and the other in 1989–90. During the first of these I received fellowship support from the John Simon Guggenheim Memorial Foundation, and during the second I was aided by a fellowship from the National Endowment for the Humanities as well as a University of California President's Research Fellowship in the Humanities. I spent the Hilary and Trinity Terms of 1990 as a Visiting Fellow of All Souls College, Oxford, and I am grateful to the Warden and Fellows for their hospitality.

I am indebted to all those who participated in the seminars I taught at Berkeley in the winter of 1983, the spring of 1986, and the fall of 1990, as well as to audiences and respondents at various other universities and conference settings over the years. Of particular value were weeklong visits to New York University in 1988 and the University of California at Riverside in 1989. In addition, a number of people read the manuscript at one stage or another and offered helpful comments. I am especially grateful to Ronald Dworkin, Thomas Nagel, Derek Parfit, Joseph Raz, and Bernard Williams.

An earlier version of chapter 2 appeared in the *Journal of Philosophy* (volume 83 [1986]: 531–37). Portions of chapters 4 and 5 have been taken, with some modifications, from a paper entitled "Naturalism, Psychoanalysis, and Moral Motivation," which is to appear in *Psychoanalysis, Mind, and Art: Perspectives on Richard Wollheim,* edited by Anthony Savile and James Hopkins (forthcoming from Basil Blackwell). Permission of the publishers to make use of material from these two papers is gratefully acknowledged.

Berkeley, Calif.   S. S.
October 1991

CONTENTS

HUMAN MORALITY

ONE

Introductory Themes

Some people think—and some great philosophers have held—that the demands of morality, properly understood, coincide with the requirements of an enlightened self-interest. For such people the most important questions about the relationship between morality and the individual concern the proper understanding of morality's demands, the individual's interests, and the character of the coincidence between them.

For those who view morality and the interests of the individual as capable of diverging, a different set of questions arises. How sharp and how frequent are the conflicts between morality and self-interest? Do such conflicts admit of any uniform theoretical resolution? In particular, do considerations of reason or rationality consistently favor one side or the other, or is it the case instead that neither morality nor self-interest is always rationally dominant? And however things may be in theory, what are the realistic prospects for morality in our social world, given the motivational power that considerations of self-interest appear to have for most people? The answers that one gives to these questions will depend on one's more detailed conception of the relation between the moral point of view and the point of view of the individual agent. For to say that considerations of morality and self-interest do not always coincide is still to leave many of the most important questions about that relation open.

Some people regard the two points of view as mutually antagonistic. They see the moral point of view as insisting on a life of austerity

3

and self-denial, while the individual's point of view recommends a life of personal fulfillment achieved through the development and exercise of a wide range of talents and capacities. My own belief, by contrast, is that the moral point of view and the point of view of the individual agent stand in a relation that might be termed one of *potential congruence*. This notion involves three constituent ideas. The first is that although moral concerns do not always coincide with considerations of the individual agent's interests, moral norms do serve to regulate the conduct of human beings, and their content is constrained by their regulative role: they must be capable of being integrated in a coherent and attractive way into an individual human life. The second idea is that, despite the undeniable strength of self-interested motives. powerful motivations that are responsive to moral considerations can also emerge during the course of an individual's development, motivations deeply rooted in the structure of the individual's personality. Moreover, these motivations help shape the interests of those who possess them, and while their existence does not guarantee that conflicts between morality's demands and the agent's interests will never arise, neither do they always work to the long-term disadvantage of their possessors. The third idea is that it is, to a large extent, a practical social task—and a practicable social goal—to achieve a measure of fit between what morality demands and what people's motivational resources can supply. For what morality demands depends on the state of the world in morally relevant respects, and what people are motivated to do depends on how they have been educated and socialized; and these factors in turn are dependent, in obvious ways, on the structure and functioning of society.

My aim in this book is to elaborate and defend this view of the relation between morality and the individual. As I have indicated, it is a view that stands intermediate between two more extreme positions: between the view that morality and self-interest ultimately coincide, and the view that they are diametrically opposed. The very structure of an intermediate position can make it difficult to defend. For since such a position compromises between two extremes, it in effect concedes some merit to each, thereby undermining its ability to employ certain of the arguments that the extremes use against each other. And since it commits itself fully to neither extreme, it in effect concedes some weakness in each, thereby undermining its ability to employ certain of the arguments that the extreme positions rely on for support. At worst an intermediate position may seem vulnerable to a charge of inconsistency or theoretical instability. At best it may seem incapable either of defending itself or of criticizing the extreme alternatives with anything like the kind of force and conviction that each of them can muster. On the other hand, intermediate positions sometimes have the most important virtue of all—the virtue of being correct. I will argue that this is such a case. Or, more accurately, I will argue that, when compared with the relevant alternatives, the view of morality I wish to defend makes better overall sense of our sometimes conflicting attitudes about the nature of moral concerns and the place of such concerns in our lives.

I will elaborate my view of the relation between morality and the individual gradually, through a discussion of questions concerning morality's content, authority, scope, and deliberative role. A unified treatment of all four of these topics is necessary in order to achieve an adequate understanding of the relation between the two perspectives. This point may be illustrated through an example, which will be discussed in greater detail in the next chapter, and which will serve to structure the argument of the book as a whole. Suppose that morality as represented by a certain philosophical theory strikes us as too demanding in what it requires of people. Does this, in principle, provide the basis for a legitimate objection, either to the theory or to morality itself? If so, is the problem that the theory has distorted the content of morality? Or is it that morality itself is excessively demanding, so that while the theory may be an accurate representation of the content of morality, people have reason to treat moral considerations as less weighty or authoritative than we may previously have supposed? Or might we instead take the position that certain areas of human life are not subject to moral demands at all—are off limits to morality—and that the theory in question may therefore be acceptable, provided that appropriate limits are placed on its scope and thereby on the extent of its demands? And what is the relation between the idea that a theory is too demanding, and the idea that it assigns too large a role to moral considerations in our thoughts and deliberations? Only through a unified approach to questions of content, authority, scope, and deliberative role can a considered view of the relation between morality and the individual emerge. Yet influential discussions of that relation have all too often failed even to distinguish clearly among these four aspects of morality, with the result that the upshot of such discussions remains obscure in crucial respects.

As far as the issue of content is concerned, I will argue that morality should be thought of as *moderate* rather than *stringent*. By this I mean that, although moral considerations and considerations of self-interest can diverge, and although morality sometimes requires significant sacrifices of us, nevertheless the most demanding moral theories are mistaken.[1] I will argue that disagreement over whether morality should be seen as moderate or stringent has its roots in a conflict between two different ideals of morality. The claim of moderation grows out of an ideal according to which morality is, from the standpoint of the individual agent, fundamentally a reasonable and humane phenomenon, despite the demands that it makes. By contrast, the claim of stringency grows out of an ideal according to which morality enjoys a more thoroughgoing independence from the perspective of the individual agent. This ideal importantly attributes to morality a kind of purity: morality's concerns are highly distinctive and sharply opposed to the self-interested concerns of the individual. I will sometimes refer to these two ideals as the Ideal of Humanity and the Ideal of Purity, respectively. Although each of them represents a strand of belief that occupies a recognizable place in our thinking about morality, I will argue that the Ideal of Humanity coheres better with more of our firmly held values and considered convictions.

With regard to the question of scope, I will argue against the view that some areas of life are immune to moral assessment. That view is often taken by people who are sympathetic to the Ideal of Humanity, but who see the demandingness of morality as mitigated by restrictions on its scope rather than by moderation in its content. I will argue, however, that moderation represents the best expression of the Ideal of Humanity, and that restrictions on the scope of morality are in the end untenable. Thus, morality should be thought of as moderate but *pervasive,* in the sense that no voluntary human action is in principle resistant to moral assessment.

---

1. My use of the term 'moderate' is inspired by, though it differs significantly from, Shelly Kagan's use of the same term in *The Limits of Morality* (Oxford: Clarendon Press, 1989). The most important difference is that, in my usage, there is room for disagreement about what specific structure morality has if it is moderate, whereas Kagan defines the term more narrowly, so that it refers to the specific view that morality includes both what he calls "options" and what he calls "constraints."

As far as the authority of morality is concerned, I will express doubts about the traditional view that morality is *overriding,* where that is understood to mean that it can never be rational knowingly to do what morality forbids. However, I will also maintain that many common arguments against overridingness are inconclusive, and more important, that less may turn on the issue of overridingness than some have supposed. For even if morality were overriding, it still would not have as much authority as some would like it to have. And even if it is not overriding, it may nevertheless have more authority than some have feared. I will suggest that support for this second claim may be provided by a psychologically realistic account of the role that moral concerns and their sources have in the range of actual human personalities. In order to make good this suggestion, however, I will need to engage a general doubt about "psychologistic" or "naturalistic" accounts of moral motivation, a doubt most powerfully expressed by Kant, who argued with great force that our own prephilosophical understanding of the authority of morality is incompatible with the idea that our motivations for behaving morally derive ultimately from our natural attitudes or from features of our psychology. Although naturalistic accounts have become more sophisticated in certain respects since Kant expressed his objections, and although they are congenial to the scientific temper of our time, I believe that they have also remained dissatisfying because they have failed to come adequately to grips with Kant's criticism. I will explore the possibility that, up to a certain point at least, the feature of typical naturalistic accounts that renders them incompatible with our prephilosophical understanding of the authority of morality is not their naturalism, but rather their psychological superficiality. Accordingly, I will suggest that it may be possible to reconcile a more sophisticated naturalistic view with at least some elements of that understanding.

Finally, with regard to morality's deliberative role, I will attempt to indicate the complex and varied ways in which it is appropriate for moral considerations to impinge on the processes by which we decide what to do. Some recent writers on this subject have objected to one model of the deliberative role of morality as overly intrusive and moralistic, as requiring us always to have explicitly moral thoughts uppermost in our minds. Such writers have sometimes seen the repudiation of the moralistic model as requiring a radically reduced conception, not only of morality's deliberative role, but also

7

of its scope, and of the possibility of any systematic moral theory as well. As against these writers, I will argue that a significant deliberative role can be ascribed to morality without relying on the moralistic model; that the ascription to morality of such a role is in fact truer to the phenomena than is the moralistic model itself; and that the ascription of such a role does not generate restrictions on the scope of morality, or require us to abandon the idea of a moral theory.

Taken together, these accounts of morality's content, scope, authority, and deliberative role, which will occupy chapters 2 through 7, will provide support for the first two of the three ideas associated with the suggestion that the relation between the moral and individual perspectives is one of potential congruence. The third idea, namely, that it is in part a social and political task to achieve a measure of fit between what morality demands and what people's motivational resources can supply, will be developed in the final chapter.

In setting out my views, one of the themes I will be concerned to emphasize, as I have already intimated, is the importance for moral philosophy of some tolerably realistic understanding of human motivational psychology. As we all know, human beings are motivated by things like sexual jealousy, blind rage, and personal loathing; by desires for revenge, recognition, and relaxation; by fears of rejection, of loss, and of death; by feelings of worthlessness and grandiosity; by the need for control and the fear of powerlessness; by the need for love and the fear of needing; by the urge to destroy and the desire to repair. However, moral philosophy has too often been content to work with a very limited and highly stylized repertoire of motivations: a repertoire that typically includes feelings of self-love and sympathy, possibly a sense of duty, and beyond that perhaps a few personal loyalties and attachments. Although a livelier sense of the possibilities may not be necessary for every purpose, I am convinced that the discussion of some of the central questions of moral philosophy could only benefit from a more serious attention to psychological reality.

This conviction represents one of several affinities between my views and the views of those many philosophers who have, in recent years, expressed dissatisfaction with the traditional Kantian and utilitarian positions that have dominated contemporary ethical theory. But despite these affinities, and despite my respect for the challenges that these critics have mounted to the conventional

8

agenda of contemporary moral philosophy, my overall view is in many ways closer to the traditional outlooks than to the position of the critics. For although I agree that the traditional views have tended to overemphasize certain abstract moral notions, such as 'right' and 'ought', and to neglect other important moral ideas,[2] I do not, as some of the critics do, regard the abstract notions themselves as inherently flawed or dispensable. And although I agree that traditional moral theorists have sometimes pressed justificatory questions in ethics beyond the point where they can reasonably be answered, I think that there is much to be gained from pursuing such questions as far as one can, and I do not regard the justificatory enterprise itself as misguided or as bereft, in the late twentieth century, of the intellectual context necessary to render it coherent. Similarly, although I agree that traditional moral philosophy has tended to exaggerate the role of rules and principles in our moral thought and experience, and to underestimate the role of individual judgment and insight, I believe that rules and principles do have their place, and that individual judgment, important as it is, is not a substitute for rules but rather plays a role that is complementary to theirs. And while it is likewise true that those who have emphasized rules have sometimes failed to appreciate the importance of the emotions in moral life, I do not believe that such appreciation is incompatible with a continued recognition of the importance of rules and principles.

Whereas some critics have taken contemporary moral theorizing to be rooted in a set of Enlightenment values and ideals that cannot ultimately be sustained, and have urged a return to older traditions of moral thought,[3] I believe that those Enlightenment values include some of the most precious elements of our moral inheritance, and that any wholesale repudiation of them not only would be unwarranted but would be tantamount to a form of moral self-destruction.

---

2. This is one of the important themes of Bernard Williams's *Ethics and the Limits of Philosophy* (Cambridge, Mass.: Harvard University Press, 1985). See also G. E. M. Anscombe, "Modern Moral Philosophy," *Philosophy* 33 (1958): 1–19.

3. See, for example, Alasdair MacIntyre, *After Virtue,* 2nd ed. (Notre Dame, Ind.: University of Notre Dame Press, 1984). In *Ethics and the Limits of Philosophy* Bernard Williams argues that contemporary moral thinking is misguided and that the ideas of the Greeks "may have more to offer" (p. 198), although at the same time he wishes to retain certain characteristically modern moral ideas and values. This produces a considerable tension in his position, as I have argued at length in "Morality Through Thick and Thin," *The Philosophical Review* 96 (1987): 411–34.

Consider, for example, the Enlightenment legacy of inclusion: the pressure generated within mainstream Western moral thought, by ideas central to Enlightenment philosophical systems, to affirm unequivocally that all human beings—including women, non-Westerners, non-Christians, and nonwhites—enjoy full moral standing. Both Kantian and utilitarian outlooks exert such pressure since each picks out, as the basis for moral standing, a property—sentience in the case of utilitarianism and rationality in the case of Kantian thought—that is manifestly not restricted to any one sex, to the members of any one racial or religious group, or to the inhabitants of any one geographical region. It has taken a long time for the inclusive implications of Enlightenment ideas to be fully recognized and absorbed, and even today the process is far from complete. Indeed, one question we now face is what would count as completing it. Here the Kantian and utilitarian criteria pull in different directions, with the Kantian emphasis on rationality making it seem plausible that only human beings enjoy full moral standing, while the utilitarian focus on sentience and related properties creates pressure for the inclusion of nonhuman animals as well. But if the process has not yet been completed, it has nevertheless had a revolutionary impact on Western moral thought, despite the fierce resistance it has encountered, and the staggering violence and brutality that have been perpetrated by those committed to reversing it.

I doubt that many readers of this book would be happy to contemplate such a reversal. Thus, when we hear longings expressed for the kind of moral coherence that is said to have characterized traditional, hierarchically ordered societies with clearly defined systems of social roles, we would do well to remember that the inclusiveness of modern morality, along with many of the other values it expresses, and that we rightly cherish, had no place whatsoever in those societies. Nor could they have had such a place without undermining the very features of those societies that have made them the objects of such intense moral nostalgia. The lesson, it seems to me, is that if, as is certainly the case, we can no longer accept certain Enlightenment ideas without significant alteration or modification, then the important question is how to effect the necessary changes while preserving those portions of the Enlightenment legacy that matter most to us. The need to answer this question presents us with the sort of task that any tradition of thought must sooner or later face if it is to endure and grow; and so it seems to me curious that some would invoke the importance of tradition as a reason for turning away from this task and attempting to recapture the moral thought of a world to which few of us could harbor any serious wish to return.[4]

In view of these remarks, it will come as no surprise to learn that I will not be aligning myself with those writers who in recent years have been urging the superiority of ancient ethical ideas over modern ones. I will not be arguing that what we need is an "ethics of virtue," nor will I be promoting a revival of Aristotelian ethical thought. In saying this, I do not mean to disparage the ideas of the ancients in any way, or to suggest that moral philosophy can safely ignore Aristotle. On the contrary, Aristotle is by any measure one of the very few towering figures in the history of ethics,[5] and we have much to learn from the ethical ideas of the Greeks. For example, it is unquestionably illuminating, as Bernard Williams has recently emphasized,[6] to compare our conceptions of agency and responsibility with those of the early Greeks, whose worldview, by virtue of its nonreligious character, and despite its reliance on supernatural categories, is closer than one might expect to modern naturalistic outlooks. My disagreement is only with those who believe that the proper remedy for the defects of contemporary moral theories is a substantial repudiation of modern moral thought in favor of some conception inspired by the ideas of the ancients. I believe, by contrast, that modern moral thought, for all its flaws, is responsible for some of the features of our social world in which we can take the greatest pride, and that its flaws should not blind us to the enormous stake that we have in the values it embodies.

On a related point, some writers who have been heavily influenced by Aristotle and by Wittgenstein have objected to the emphasis that contemporary moral philosophy has placed on moral theorizing: on the attempt to establish the superiority of some set of

4. For a related discussion of "postmodernist" attacks on Enlightenment ideas, see Sabina Lovibond, "Feminism and Postmodernism," *New Left Review* 178 (1989): 5–25.

5. The importance for moral philosophy of Aristotle's thought is a prominent theme in the writings of G. E. M. Anscombe, Philippa Foot, Stuart Hampshire, Alasdair MacIntyre, John McDowell, and David Wiggins, among others.

6. He made this point in his Sather Lectures delivered at the University of California at Berkeley in the spring semester of 1989. A revised version of those lectures will appear as *Shame and Necessity* (Berkeley: University of California Press, 1993).

general and universal moral principles. This emphasis is said to depend on a confusion about rationality, and it is contrasted with an emphasis on the role in our lives of shared sensitivities that cannot be codified in any set of principles, but that manifest themselves instead in the appreciation of particular cases.[7] In a somewhat similar vein, some have criticized mainstream moral philosophy for its endless demands for justification, its seemingly unsatisfiable thirst for reasons, its apparent insistence on meeting any proposed justification of one of the practices we engage in or one of the distinctions we rely on with a demand for some further defense of the putatively justifying ideas themselves. Such an insistence, it is said, betrays a failure to recognize that at some point our capacity to provide reasons for our practices or for the distinctions we rely on must give out. The chain of reasons must terminate in some set of ideas or way of life that makes sense to us, but that cannot itself be given a discursive justification or supported by an appeal to any further principle.

These objections raise deep issues about rationality, justification, and the nature of human cognitive activity. However, there are two important points that have not, in my view, been taken seriously enough by those who have pressed such objections. The first has to do with the role of moral principles in social and political life. The articulation and discussion of such principles within a society provides a shared reference point for the formulation and adjudication of challenges to existing configurations of power and privilege, and to existing social institutions and practices more generally. Ideally, it provides a public standard of accountability to which everyone has access and from which nobody is exempt. Any person, no matter how poor, or powerless, or socially marginal, no matter how remote from the centers of influence and privilege, may, by invoking moral principles, assert a claim or express a grievance in the language of a system to which nobody, however rich, powerful, or well-bred, may claim immunity. In this way the public articulation of such principles reflects the democratic character of the moral point of view and reveals the illegitimacy of any attempted privatization of moral standards, that is, of any claim by an elite to have a privileged access to moral ideas or to the moral truth. The notion that moral principles can have these functions does not rest on any confusion

---

7. See, in this connection, John McDowell, "Virtue and Reason," *The Monist* 62 (1979): 331–50.

about rationality, nor, as I have already asserted and as I will argue in chapter 3, is it in any way incompatible with a full acknowledgment of the indispensable roles of individual sensitivity, judgment, and perceptiveness in moral thought.

The second point is that the justificatory enterprise in which much contemporary moral philosophy has been engaged is itself a practice, and one that is closely linked with larger social practices of moral inquiry and debate. These practices, like any others, must be judged in part by their results and their roles in people's lives. And what is striking about these particular practices is the way in which they give expression to fundamental social values of truthfulness, accountability, openmindedness, and rational equality. This does not, of course, mean that the justificatory ambitions of those engaged in the practices cannot legitimately be subject to philosophical criticism. On the other hand, charges of justificatory excess are not themselves immune to challenge. It bears saying that the fact that justification must come to an end somewhere does not mean that a demand for justification can appropriately be ignored whenever it would be awkward or indeed impossible to respond to it. The fact that justification must terminate in something does not mean that it always terminates precisely where we would like it to, nor does it mean that nothing is ever unjustified. And although it is undeniable that participants in the justificatory enterprise sometimes display a dialectical zeal that is philosophically and humanly excessive, nevertheless the critical dialectic has been an important instrument of social change, and the justificatory enterprise has been and continues to be an important source of pressure against unjust and inhumane policies, practices, and institutions. The more urgent worry is not that too much justificatory pressure is being exerted, but rather that such pressure is not powerful enough to oppose the existing forces of inhumanity and evil.

I have been suggesting that the repudiation of contemporary moral theorizing in favor of an earlier set of ethical ideas has some strikingly conservative implications, and places a variety of progressive moral values in serious jeopardy. For some conservative critics, of course, this is precisely the point of the criticism, but there are other critics whose aims are not conservative, and who in my view have failed to come fully to terms with this aspect of the issue. Because the focus has been on the failings of contemporary moral ideas, questions about the precise character of any proposed alternative have been pressed less urgently, and the radical diversity of political and social orientation among the critics has remained in the background of the discussion. But it is noteworthy that the opposition to contemporary moral theorizing has in fact produced some rather odd alliances: between conservative traditionalists and progressive communitarians, for example, and between a refined English Aristotelianism and a moral orientation with roots in the American counterculture of the late sixties. These are oversimplifications, of course, but they rightly suggest that there are those among the critics who, although they have found certain aspects of Aristotle's view genuinely congenial, and although they have sometimes embraced "virtue ethics" as a rallying point for opposition to contemporary ideas, have nevertheless been motivated less by a belief in the superiority of some earlier model than by a conviction that modern ideas are inadequate. More specifically, contemporary moral thought has seemed to these critics to ignore a number of important features of moral life, including the moral significance of friendship and close personal relations more generally, the importance of the emotions in moral thought and practice, and the values associated with membership in a genuine community. In effect, these critics have seen contemporary moral thought as reflecting the impersonality and lack of human sensitivity that seem to characterize so much of modern life. And this type of criticism has lately been reinforced, and to some extent recast, by an influential strand of feminist moral theory, according to which the emphasis in contemporary thought on abstract moral rules and on quasi-juridical concepts such as those of duty, obligation, and justice is the result of a deeply entrenched gender bias, which also explains the relative neglect of the moral significance of the emotions and of close personal relations.[8]

It is, of course, a commonplace of contemporary social commentary that the conditions of life in modern Western societies are such that many people no longer feel strongly identified with any particular group, community, or cultural tradition, and that this has given rise to a host of social and psychological maladies, since there is nothing else in modern life that has managed successfully to play the

---

8. The most widely discussed formulation of this argument is presented in Carol Gilligan's *In a Different Voice* (Cambridge, Mass.: Harvard University Press, 1982), although Gilligan's special concern is with the bias she perceives in traditional psychological theories of moral development.

role heretofore played by such identifications. The causes of this state of affairs are obviously complex and open to different inter- pretations, but by any account the explosive growth of scientific knowledge in modern times must surely be one of the major factors, since it is the rise of a broadly scientific worldview that has served to undermine the systems of belief around which so many commu- nities and religious and cultural traditions have been organized. Even those who would now repudiate that worldview cannot recapture the epistemic position of earlier believers, for those early believers did not themselves need to repudiate science in order to hold the beliefs that they did. They were not in the position of affirming traditional beliefs despite or in the face of conflicting scientific evidence. Their beliefs were not the product of epistemological defiance, and their prescientific innocence cannot be recaptured.

If this is right, then the gravity of the modern predicament can hardly be overstated. On the one hand, the rise of modern science could not now be undone by anything other than a catastrophe of world-historical proportions, and in any case few could seriously wish to undo it. On the other hand, membership in communities and participation in cultural and religious traditions can clearly serve to provide people with ways of interpreting the significance of their existence and ways of understanding their relations to the social and natural worlds that are of incalculable value to them and enrich their lives beyond measure.[9] The void created when there is nothing to play these roles is both terrifying and potentially dangerous. Thus few challenges in modern life are more important than the challenge of creating forms of community, and of developing new or modified traditions of culture or religion (or its analogues), that will be capable, compatibly with our overall system of beliefs and with the conditions of the modern world, of enriching our lives in the way that earlier communities and traditions enriched the lives of earlier generations. But it would be a mistake to suppose that this requires anything like a wholesale repudiation of modern moral ideas. It may well be that the significance of certain values has been neglected in

---

9. Contemporary discussions of the importance of "communitarian" values may be found in MacIntyre's *After Virtue* and Michael Sandel's *Liberalism and the Limits of Justice* (Cambridge: Cambridge University Press, 1982), as well as in the writings of Charles Taylor and Michael Walzer, among others. On the moral importance of friendship, see for example Lawrence Blum, *Friendship, Altruism, and Morality* (London: Routledge and Kegan Paul, 1980).

contemporary moral philosophy, and that modern moral ideas need to be supplemented in various ways. But there is a world of difference between supplementation and substitution, and I see no reason to think that the values of friendship, community, and tradition can take the place of more abstract moral notions like fairness, social justice, and the equal worth of persons. After all, communities can be suffocating and oppressive, traditions can license cruelty and intolerance, and close personal relationships can be destructive and exploitative. Modern moral ideas provide us with a vantage point from which particular human relationships and practices can be criticized in the name of humanity itself; it is a vantage point that we have attained slowly and imperfectly, and one that is not easily sustained. I do not think that we do ourselves any favors by repudiating it, and I believe that we have every reason for aspiring to forms of friendship, community, and tradition that are consistent with more abstract moral values.[10] Similarly, feminist moral critics are surely correct when they suggest that those who articulate moral ideas are no likelier than anyone else to be free from various forms of cultural bias. Yet in attempting to correct for the particular forms of bias to which feminist critics have called attention, we should take care to preserve those modern moral values that remain defensible and deserve our allegiance—indeed, that have helped to create the moral climate in which feminist thought itself has flourished. For example, we should not forget the Enlightenment legacy of inclusion or the extent to which modern conceptions of justice and equality provide premises to which many feminist arguments explicitly or implicitly appeal.

In this book I will not try to offer any direct defense of the very broad perspective that I have been sketching in the last several pages. My primary purpose in sketching it has been to explain the differences between my orientation and that of certain other writers who have offered criticisms of the leading contemporary theories with which I am in many ways sympathetic. At the same time, this broad point of view does underlie the conception of morality I will be defending. Thus, to the extent that it is persuasive, that conception may serve as a partial recommendation of the broader perspective.

---

10. For related discussions, see Amy Gutmann, "Communitarian Critics of Liberalism," *Philosophy and Public Affairs* 14 (1985): 308–22, and Susan Moller Okin, *Justice, Gender, and the Family* (New York: Basic Books, 1989).

TWO

Morality's Demands and Their Limits: Competing Views

How much does morality demand of individuals? In a world where human misery and suffering exist on a vast scale, and where acts that are atrocities on any plausible view come to our attention daily, the theoretical and practical importance of this question is evident. In recent years some of the leading traditional moral theories have been criticized as excessively demanding. It is by no means clear, however, what kind of force such criticisms have.

If an otherwise plausible normative moral theory makes unusually heavy demands of individual moral agents, what is the appropriate response to that theory? Here are four possibilities. The first is to say that the theory is unacceptable, and that we should seek a less demanding one. The second is to say that certain areas of human life are simply not subject to moral assessment or moral demands, so that the theory may be acceptable provided its scope is construed as restricted, with the severity of its demands limited in consequence. The third response holds that morality itself is extremely demanding, that the theory in question may thus be entirely acceptable as a theory of what morality requires, but that because morality is so demanding its authority is limited, in the sense that it is sometimes rational for people to ignore its injunctions. The fourth response denies that the demandingness of the theory suggests any flaw or limitation, either in the theory or in morality itself. Morality may be very demanding, and so any adequate moral theory may have to be very demanding, too. But this is no objection to either. Morality demands what it demands, and if people find it difficult to live up to

17

those demands, that only shows what everyone knows anyway: that people are not, in general, morally very good.

Of these four responses, the first two and the last two may be thought of as pairs. What the first two have in common is the idea that what morality demands is limited by considerations having to do with the individual agent's psychology and well-being. They disagree about whether the limitations are built into the content of morality or whether they operate instead as restrictions on its scope, but they agree that there *are* limitations. The third and fourth responses, by contrast, deny this. Morality demands what it demands, they assert, and it may in fact demand a great deal. Of course we may find it hard to satisfy the demands of morality. So much the worse for morality, says the third response. So much the worse for us, says the fourth.

The first and second responses may both be thought of as growing out of a view according to which morality—despite the claims of its more zealous self-appointed champions, and in distinction from the harsh and punitive judgments and feelings with which, for complicated reasons, it often becomes entangled in the course of an individual's development—is, from the standpoint of the agent, fundamentally a reasonable phenomenon. The third and fourth responses, on the other hand, may both be thought of as rooted in a conception of morality as more radically disengaged from the perspective of the individual agent—from the full range of concerns associated with the living of an actual human life. Much of this book will be concerned with the contrast between these two divergent conceptions of morality. In this chapter, however, I will begin with the smaller issue posed by the choice between the two responses that constitute the first pair. If one agrees that the demands of morality are limited by considerations having to do with the effects of those demands on individual agents, then are the relevant limitations best thought of as part of the content of morality, as the first response would have it, or as restrictions on its scope, as suggested by the second response?

Critics of the first response may say that the idea of responding to an excessively demanding moral theory by substituting a less demanding one has an intolerably moralistic cast. Although a less demanding theory would permit things that a more demanding theory would forbid, there are some cases, it may be said, in which the point is not that agents are *morally permitted* to do what the more demanding theory forbids, but rather that the issue of moral permissibility simply does not arise. Agents do not need moral permission to do certain kinds of things.[1]

In what circumstances might we be inclined to say of some act that it needed no moral permission or justification? Two kinds of examples are frequently mentioned. First, some acts are said to be too trivial to be subject to moral evaluation. It would strike us as fatuous, for instance, to claim that I was morally justified in brushing my teeth this morning. Examples of the second kind are cases in which a failure to perform some act would be extremely costly, either to the agent himself or to someone dear to him. Thus Bernard Williams discusses a case in which a man can, at no cost to himself, save the life of either but not both of two people, one of whom is his wife and the other a stranger.[2] It would be wrong, Williams says, to claim that the man is morally justified in saving his wife precisely because she is his wife. We should instead see this as a situation that "lie[s] beyond justifications."[3]

If we are concerned with the question of how to respond to an unusually demanding moral theory, examples of the second type may appear to be of more central interest to us than those of the first. For in a case like the one Williams mentions, we can imagine a very

---

1. Compare Susan Wolf:

> It is misleading to insist that one is *permitted* to live a life in which the goals, relationships, activities, and interests that one pursues are not maximally morally good. For our lives are not so comprehensively subject to the requirement that we apply for permission, and our nonmoral reasons for the goals we set ourselves are not excuses, but may rather be positive, good reasons which do not exist *despite* any reasons that might threaten to outweigh them. ("Moral Saints," *Journal of Philosophy* 79 [1982]: 436)

2. See "Persons, Character and Morality," in *Moral Luck* (New York: Cambridge University Press, 1981), pp. 1–19. The case Williams discusses was originally brought up by Charles Fried in *Right and Wrong* (Cambridge, Mass.: Harvard University Press, 1978).

3. "Persons, Character and Morality," p. 18. I am interpreting the claim that the situation is beyond justifications as meaning that the man's act of saving his wife excludes moral assessment: the issue of moral justification does not arise here. Although I believe that this interpretation represents the most natural way of understanding the passages from "Persons, Character and Morality" that I discuss in this chapter, other interpretations are possible. And there are other places, both in "Persons, Character and Morality" and elsewhere, where Williams expresses views that seem to have different implications for cases like these. Whether or not the interpretation I rely on here is the best interpretation of Williams's considered views on the matter, it represents a theoretically important position, and one to which Williams himself seems drawn at least some of the time.

demanding moral theory insisting that the fact that one of the people in danger is the man's wife does not provide him with a justification for saving her instead of the stranger. Perhaps, on some views, the man ought to flip a coin, or determine whose death would be a greater loss to humanity, or whatever. Thus the question of whether the man is more plausibly seen as justified in saving his wife or as needing no justification at all may naturally be thought of as a question about how best to respond to a very demanding moral theory.[4] By contrast, it seems hard to imagine that there is any sane view according to which I was morally unjustified in brushing my teeth this morning. So while there is still a question about whether to say that I was morally justified in brushing my teeth this morning, or to say instead that I did not need a moral justification, this question seems less directly related to issues about demandingness.

Nevertheless, I think it pays to consider the two types of case together, for two reasons. First, as I will argue shortly, most moral views will in fact want to say that brushing one's teeth is at least sometimes morally impermissible; if so, it may not after all be so farfetched to suppose that questions about the degree of morality's demandingness can arise in connection with cases of this kind. Second and more important, the considerations that bear on the issue of whether to construe the realm of the permissible as extending to trivial cases, and the considerations that bear on the issue of whether to construe that realm as extending to desperate cases like Williams's, are, as I will again argue shortly, fundamentally the same.

Does it, then, seem correct to say that acts like my brushing my teeth and acts like the man's saving his wife exclude moral assessment? We can begin by asking why, exactly, it may strike some people as intolerably moralistic to think of acts of these two types as being morally permissible. There may be a clue in Williams's response to the question whether the fact that one of the people is the

4. This does not mean that every demanding theory would in this case deny that the man was justified in saving his wife. A deontological theory that was in general quite demanding might in this example say that the man was *required* to save his wife. Thus a theory may be very demanding on the whole without making burdensome demands in every situation. On the relation between the overall demandingness of a theory and its demandingness for particular agents on particular occasions, see pp. 98–99. For a context in which a requirement to save his wife might itself, exceptionally, be very demanding for the man in Williams's example, see p. 24.

man's wife might not provide a justification for his deciding to save her instead of the stranger:

> It depends on how much weight is carried by 'justification': the consideration that it was his wife is certainly, for instance, an explanation which should silence comment. But something more ambitious than this is usually intended, essentially involving the idea that moral principle can legitimate his preference, yielding the conclusion that in situations of this kind it is at least all right (morally permissible) to save one's wife. . . . But this construction provides the agent with one thought too many: it might have been hoped by some (for instance, by his wife) that his motivating thought, fully spelled out, would be the thought that it was his wife, not that it was his wife and that in situations of this kind it is permissible to save one's wife.[5]

On one natural reading of this passage, Williams is making a strong assumption: he is assuming, on this reading, that if we deem it morally permissible for the man to save his wife precisely because she *is* his wife, we are then committed to a further view about what the man's "motivating thought" should be when he acts; his motivating thought should be that it is his wife who is in danger, and that in such situations it is morally permissible to save one's wife. Given this strong assumption, the view that it is permissible for the man to save his wife may well seem intolerably moralistic. Similarly, the view that it was permissible for me to brush my teeth this morning may indeed seem objectionable, if it implies that I ought to have been motivated in brushing, even in part, by the thought that it was permissible for me to do so.

We must therefore ask whether the strong assumption is correct. If so, we may be inclined to agree that there are certain kinds of action that it would be intolerably moralistic to classify as morally permissible. As we have seen, the strong assumption makes use of the idea of the man's "motivating thought, fully spelled out." And it must be said that the notion of a "motivating thought" is not altogether clear, still less so the notion of a "motivating thought, fully spelled out." Let us suppose, however, as seems reasonable in the context of the passage as a whole, that such a thought must be one that the man actually has, as opposed, say, to one that he would have, if the justifiability of his action were challenged. Then, al-

5. Ibid., p. 18.

though there may perhaps be philosophical views from which the strong assumption, so interpreted, follows, that assumption is bound to strike most people, upon reflection, as very implausible.[6] It is implausible to suppose that, in general, whenever one makes a favorable assessment of the moral permissibility of an act, one is committed to saying that the agent who performs the act ought to have, and ought in part to be motivated by, the thought of its permissibility. Nor is there is anything about the specific act Williams is discussing that would explain why a favorable assessment of the permissibility of that particular act does indeed commit one to such a claim.[7] Note how farfetched a parallel assumption about prudential evaluations would be: we might think that it was in the man's own interest to save his wife, but that would hardly commit us to the claim that it was in his interest to be motivated in saving her by the thought that it was in his interest to do so.

Of course, since morality has an important action-guiding function, it is presumably desirable that moral evaluations should sometimes enter into agents' deliberations about what to do. So even if we insist that one can make a favorable moral assessment of an act without being committed to the claim that the agent who performs the act ought to be motivated by that very assessment, there remains an important general question about the circumstances in which it is appropriate for moral assessments to impinge upon deliberation. Moreover, other readings are possible of the passage from Williams's paper that I have quoted, and they provide other possible

---

6. Some might interpret Kant as being committed to something like the strong assumption. That such an interpretation would not be correct is suggested by Barbara Herman's "Integrity and Impartiality" (*The Monist* 66 [1983]: 233–50), which contains a discussion of the passage from Williams's article that I have quoted.

7. It is interesting to compare Williams's discussion of the rescue case with some comments he has made elsewhere: "The importance of an ethical concept need not lie in its being itself an element of first-person deliberation. The deliberations of people who are generous or brave . . . are different from the deliberations of those who are not like that, but the difference does not mainly lie in their thinking about themselves in terms of generosity or courage" (*Ethics and the Limits of Philosophy* [Cambridge, Mass.: Harvard University Press, 1985], p. 11).

Of course Williams thinks that the concept of moral permissibility is in various respects unlike "thick" ethical concepts, such as the concepts of generosity and courage. And so, in various respects, it may be. This much is nevertheless true: the importance of the concept of moral permissibility is not exhausted by its role in first-personal deliberation. (I have made some more general remarks about Williams's contrast between "thick" ethical concepts and others in "Morality Through Thick and Thin," *The Philosophical Review* 96 [1987]: 411–34.)

interpretations of what he thinks we commit ourselves to when we formulate a moral assessment of someone's action. As this suggests, there also remains a legitimate question about whether, when we formulate an assessment of someone else's action, we commit ourselves to *any* view about what the content of that person's thoughts should be. I will consider these questions in the next chapter. For the present, it suffices to reiterate that the strong assumption is very implausible. Thus the charge that the first response to the demandingness criticism is excessively moralistic may be unsupported, insofar as it depends on a generalized form of that assumption. Of course the most that we accomplish, if we succeed in rebutting that charge, is to eliminate some of the motivation for the second response. It remains to supply some positive reason for preferring one response or the other.

Consider again trivial actions. There certainly seems to be some plausibility to the claim that some acts are not important enough to warrant moral assessment. This is partly because it can seem hard to imagine what—other than philosophical discussion—would lead anyone actually to say or even to think that, for example, it was morally permissible for me to brush my teeth this morning. It may seem hard to supply that evaluative proposition with a plausible setting in ordinary human thought and discourse. But suppose that, as I began to brush, some food lodged in the windpipe of the person in the next room. Through the open door I saw the person trying vainly to dislodge the food. I realized what was happening, I am expert in the use of the Heimlich maneuver, and I knew that there was nobody else in a position to help. If I nevertheless proceeded to brush merrily away, then I presumably did something morally unacceptable. This suggests that, when we agreed that my brushing my teeth this morning seemed too trivial to warrant moral assessment, we were taking it for granted that nobody was choking to death in the next room as I was brushing, and that there was no comparable emergency that I was in a comparably good position to respond to. More generally, the judgment that a particular act is "too trivial" to warrant moral evaluation implicitly depends on an assessment not only of the act itself, but also of the consequences of the act, the alternatives available to the agent, and their consequences. For ease of discussion, and not as a claim with any independent meaning, we can summarize this by saying that such a judgment always depends implicitly on an assessment of the act and its context.

Thus the judgment that a particular act is too trivial to warrant moral evaluation always depends on an assessment of the act and its context. And for any given act that is said to be too trivial, we can imagine a change of context that would render it suitable for moral evaluation. If these two points are correct, I can see no basis for distinguishing between acts that are morally permissible and those that are too trivial to warrant moral evaluation. For there is no relevant difference between the kind of assessment that issues in judgments of triviality and the kind that issues in judgments of moral permissibility, prohibition, and requirement. Both consist in assessment of the act and its context, and both are sensitive to the same sorts of features. It is tempting to conclude that a judgment of triviality constitutes a disguised form of moral judgment, for it appears to depend on an assessment of the act and its context that is indistinguishable from moral assessment. At the very least, the distinction between morally permissible acts and those too trivial to evaluate seems to multiply categories needlessly, for it is unclear what the putative distinction comes to. In each case the acts in question are regarded as acceptable, in the sense that they are neither morally required nor morally prohibited. Assignment of an act to either category depends on the same kind of assessment of the act and its context, and the same sorts of changes in context would lead to reassignment of acts from either of these categories to one of the others.

Similar considerations apply to cases like the rescue case. Anyone familiar with the contemporary philosophical art of counterexample construction will be able to supply a context in which the man's saving his wife would be, shall we say, morally dubious. The man's wife, whom he loathes and has recently sued for divorce, is a notorious and sadistic mass murderer who will be missed by nobody. The stranger, on the other hand, is a brilliant and saintly medical researcher who, in addition to being the sole source of support for five small and adorable children plus two aged and admirable parents, has just discovered a cure for cancer but has not yet had a chance to write it down. You get the idea. Any judgment that a particular act is "beyond justifications," like a judgment of triviality, implicitly depends on an assessment of the act and its context that appears to be indistinguishable from moral assessment. And for any given act that is thought to be beyond justifications, we can imagine a change in context that would render it suitable for moral evaluation. So it is not clear what the distinction between acts that are beyond justifications and acts that are morally permissible really comes to.

A further point. I have been discussing the idea that in the original example—where we have been taking it for granted that the wife is not a loathsome murderer and the stranger is not a saintly medical researcher—the man's saving his wife is beyond justifications. I have argued that such a judgment depends implicitly on a kind of assessment of the act and its context that is indistinguishable from moral assessment. But beyond this, it is also the case that other acts available to the same agent at the same time seem uncontroversially subject to moral assessment. (What if he saved the stranger and let his wife die? Or what if he sat by, whistling and twiddling his thumbs, and watched them both die? What if he pulled out a gun and shot them both?) If this is right, then the claim that the original act does not admit of moral assessment comes to seem even less plausible—to me, at any rate.

Considerations such as these lead me to prefer the first response to the demandingness criticism over the second. They also provide support for the idea that morality is *pervasive,* in the sense that no voluntary human action is in principle resistant to moral assessment (although of course one or another of the familiar excusing conditions may apply). To say that morality is pervasive is not to claim that human action is the only thing subject to moral appraisal. Nor is it to deny that some acts warrant much finer-grained appraisal than others. And it is certainly not to deny either that there are countlessly many acts with respect to which no human being will ever engage in the *activity* of moral appraisal at all, or that that is a very good thing: there are times when it is not appropriate or healthy or humanly supportable or, for that matter, morally desirable to engage in the activity. The idea that morality is pervasive simply means that, subject to the qualification about excusing conditions that I have mentioned, all voluntary human conduct is in principle morally assessable.

The suggestion that morality is pervasive neither entails nor is entailed by the more frequently discussed claim that morality is *overriding,* where that is understood as meaning that it can never be rational knowingly to do what morality forbids. More generally, morality may be seen as having any combination of the following properties: pervasiveness, overridingness, and, as I shall refer to it, *stringency,* the property of being very demanding within whatever domain it applies.

It is easy to become confused about the difference between stringency and overridingness, for the following reason. In assessing what individuals ought morally to do, most people will agree that considerations of the agent's own interests are sometimes *overridden* by other considerations, so that what one morally ought to do sometimes differs from what would maximally advance one's own interests.[8] Since those who believe that morality is stringent see this happening more often than those who do not, stringency can be identified with the relatively frequent overriding of the agent's interests in arriving at overall moral verdicts. However the "claim of overridingness," as I am understanding it, is the very different idea that, *given* an overall verdict about what one morally ought to do, one cannot rationally defy it. The claim that morality is overriding in this sense is clearly distinct from, and independent of, the claim that it is stringent.

Although, as I have said, morality may be seen as having any combination of the three properties mentioned, people's attitudes toward any one of these properties may be affected by their beliefs about the others. For example, some who believe that morality is overriding may for that very reason be inclined to resist the suggestion that it is pervasive, feeling that the authority of morality is so great within its domain that that domain must be limited, if people are to have sufficient opportunity to pursue personal projects and commitments. Of course this concern is likely to be greatest when morality is also thought of as stringent, and then it may help to explain the appeal of what I have been calling the "second response." And it is likely to diminish if stringency is rejected, so that morality itself is construed as permitting people to devote substantial attention to personal projects. Or, to take another example, some who deny that morality is stringent may for that reason be inclined to *accept* the suggestion that it is overriding. They may feel that morality as they understand it already gives people's personal projects all the weight they can rationally have, so that, in any conflict that nevertheless arises between morality and personal concerns, the

---

8. There are of course views that deny this and disallow the possibility of conflict between morality and self-interest. I discuss such views in chapters 4 and 7.

balance of reasons must always favor morality.[9] However, they are not committed to this view. The claim of overridingness remains an independent thesis, which those who deny that morality is stringent can accept or reject.

One reaction to an unusually demanding moral theory is to deny that morality has the property of stringency, and hence to conclude that the theory in question cannot be acceptable. That, in effect, is what I have been calling the "first response." Another reaction is to deny that morality is pervasive, thus mitigating the severity of the theory's demands. That is what I have been calling the "second response." Still another reaction is to deny that morality is overriding, and so to challenge its authority, while allowing that the theory in question may be perfectly acceptable as a theory of what morality requires. That is what the third response does. Only the fourth response is compatible with the view that morality has all three properties: overridingness, pervasiveness, and stringency.

In this chapter I have defended the first response as against the second: defended the denial of stringency over the denial of pervasiveness as an expression of the idea that what morality demands is limited by considerations having to do with the individual agent's psychology and well-being. I have not, however, defended that idea itself against the opposing view, in which the third and fourth responses are both rooted, and which, as I have noted, sees morality as more radically disengaged from the standpoint of the individual agent. To put it another way: although I have expressed my sympathy for a view of morality as pervasive and nonstringent, and although I have given a general argument in favor of the idea that morality is pervasive, I have not yet given any argument against the claim of stringency. Also, I have yet to discuss the question of overridingness; for if morality may be seen as having any combination of the three properties under discussion, then of course to say that it is pervasive and nonstringent is still to leave the question of overridingness open. Moreover, although the argument for pervasiveness presented in this chapter can stand on its own, it remains important, as we have seen, to supplement that argument with a

---

9. See Thomas Nagel, *The View from Nowhere* (New York: Oxford University Press, 1986), chapter 10.

further discussion of the relations between the moral assessement of action and agents' deliberations about what to do.

This last task is the one that I will undertake in the next chapter. My consideration of overridingness, and of the authority of morality more generally, will occupy chapters 4 and 5. Chapters 6 and 7 will be devoted to a discussion and defense of the view that morality is not stringent, although it is not altogether *undemanding* either; this view I shall refer to as the view that morality is *moderate*. Taken together, the present chapter and the following five will provide an interpretation of the complex relations between the requirements of morality and the living of a human life: an interpretation, in other words, both of how and why the content of morality is constrained by considerations of the agent's psychology and well-being, and of the ways in which it is appropriate for morality to enter into an agent's life, and to impinge on his or her thought, deliberation, feeling, and action.

THREE

Assessment, Deliberation, and Theory

The claim that morality is pervasive may be resisted out of a feeling that it embodies an excessively moralistic view of human life. As we have seen, that feeling may in turn depend on the strong assumption that once one classifies an act as morally permissible, one is committed to holding that the agent who performs it should be motivated, at least in part, by the thought of its moral permissibility. Given this assumption, the claim of pervasiveness may seem to imply, not only that we ought always to act in ways that are morally acceptable, but also that we ought always to be motivated by the thought of our actions' acceptability. In this way the claim of pervasiveness may seem to bring with it an extravagantly moralistic conception of how human deliberation should proceed. Resistance to the claim may, accordingly, be generated by a distaste for that conception; it may derive from the fear of an overmoralized self.

If, as I have argued, the strong assumption is false, then the fear of an overmoralized self is unwarranted to the extent that it depends on that assumption. As we have seen, however, there remains a legitimate question about whether, when we formulate a moral assessment of someone else's action, we commit ourselves to *any* view about what the content of that person's thoughts should be. If so, then the claim that morality is pervasive may threaten to commit us to an overmoralized conception of the self, even if the strong assumption is wrong. Before taking up this question, however, it will be helpful to consider the general issue of how and when it is appropriate or desirable for moral considerations to impinge on an agent's deliberative activities.

First some terminological matters. I will call the judgment that a particular act is morally required, permissible, or prohibited an *overall moral verdict* about that act. I will treat judgments about what agents ought to do, or about what it would be right for them to do, as equivalent to judgments about what they are morally required to do. And I will treat judgments about what agents ought not to do, or about what it would be wrong for them to do, as equivalent to judgments about what they are morally prohibited from doing. Finally, it will be helpful to distinguish between a narrow use and a broad use of the term 'moral consideration'. Used narrowly, it may refer to any consideration that is cast in what would ordinarily be regarded as explicitly or overtly moral terms. In this usage, moral considerations include *verdictive* considerations about what one ought or ought not to do, about what is morally required or forbidden, and so on, as well as more specific *evidential* considerations, such as considerations of rights, fairness, equality, and the like, which support but do not constitute overall moral verdicts.[1] Used broadly, the term 'moral consideration' may refer either to a verdictive consideration or to any consideration that supports an overall moral verdict, whether or not the supporting consideration is formulated in explicitly moral terms. Consider, for example, the rescue case discussed in the previous chapter. If we suppose that it is permissible for the man to save his wife precisely because she is his wife, then the consideration that she is his wife counts as a moral consideration in the broad but not in the narrow usage. For our present purposes, the important thing to note is that, in raising the question of how moral considerations are to be conceived of as impinging on agents' deliberations, it is the role of overtly moral considerations—moral considerations narrowly understood—that we are inquiring about. For it is primarily the possibility of assigning too large a role to those considerations that generates the threat of an overly moralized conception of deliberation. With these remarks as background, let me now distinguish among five different ways in which overtly moral considerations may impinge on an agent's deliberations about what to do.[2]

1. The distinction between *verdictive* and *evidential* considerations is taken from Philippa Foot, "Are Moral Considerations Overriding?," in her *Virtues and Vices* (Berkeley: University of California Press, 1978), pp. 181–88.
2. It should be emphasized that, in drawing these distinctions, I do not mean to be addressing questions about the motivational power of beliefs as compared with

First, a person may be moved to act in response to an overall moral verdict that he arrives at as the result of explicit reflection about what he regards as the morally salient features of the situation he is in, including reflection about the general moral rules or principles he takes to be pertinent to that situation. Imagine, as an illustration, someone who withholds payment of his income taxes because he believes they would be used to help finance immoral policies, and because he decides, as a matter of principle, that withholding payment is the right thing to do.

Second, a person may be moved to act in response to an overall moral verdict arrived at after reflection involving no explicit consideration of any general rules or principles. Imagine, for example, that someone is deciding whether to visit a sick friend or to stay at home and watch a favorite television program. After thinking it over briefly, he decides that he ought to visit his friend, so that is what he does. However, at no point in his reflections does he formulate for himself any general principle, say, to the effect that when one is faced with a choice between visiting a sick friend or watching a favorite television program, one ought to do the former. He simply allows himself to experience the pull of each of the competing considerations, after which he arrives straightaway at the conclusion that visiting his friend is what he ought to do, whereupon he does it.

Third, a person may be moved to act on the basis of an overall moral verdict arrived at without any explicit reflection. Imagine that a public official is asked by an old friend to intercede on behalf of the friend's wayward brother in an ongoing legal proceeding. The official's immediate reaction is that it would be wrong for her to accede to the request, and she turns it down without further ado.

Fourth, a person may be moved to act in response to some specific feature of a situation that he sees as morally salient, that is, that he represents to himself in overtly moral terms, but without ever explicitly concluding that the feature in question supports an overall

---

desires, and nothing that I say is intended as an answer to that sort of question. I am concerned instead with the different ways in which moral considerations may enter into a person's deliberations about what to do, leaving open the question of whether the deliberative status of such considerations is best understood in purely cognitive terms, and if so, the question of whether they must be supplemented by suitable desires in order to move an agent to action. I take up questions of the latter type in chapters 4 and 5.

moral verdict requiring or permitting him to act as he does. For example, think of a physician who provides a patient with certain information because he believes that the patient is entitled to it, but who never has any mediating thought to the effect that he *ought* to provide the information to the patient.

Finally, although acting in response to some feature of a situation that he does not represent to himself in overtly moral terms, a person may nevertheless satisfy two related counterfactual conditions: first, that he would not have acted as he did if he had believed that doing so was wrong; second, that if a consideration had come to his attention that seemed to militate against the moral permissibility of his act, he would not have performed the act, unless further deliberation had convinced him that there was reason to discount the consideration in question. This category includes cases where the consideration in response to which the agent does act, although not couched in overtly moral terms, nevertheless has obvious moral relevance ("He's drowning!"), and also cases in which it does not ("This needs salt").

There is, as far as I can see, very little of a general character that can usefully be said about the respective circumstances in which it is appropriate or desirable for moral considerations to play each of these roles. There is no general rule that tells us when moral considerations should function in one of these ways and when in another, and different people may have different deliberative styles that are equally effective in producing morally exemplary behavior. This is not to say that all such styles are equally effective, or that the role of moral considerations in a person's deliberations can never be open to criticism. It is merely to say that we cannot specify any routine method for determining what deliberative role moral considerations should play in particular circumstances, and that there need not be a unique answer to that question in every situation.[3]

If someone normally succeeded in acting in ways that were morally acceptable, it would be reasonable to infer that moral considerations almost always impinged on that person's deliberations in one of the ways I have enumerated, though not of course in the same way on every occasion. This is obviously not to say, however, that if moral considerations almost always impinge on

3. For a related but more general discussion, see the Postscript to Joseph Raz's *Practical Reasons and Norms,* 2nd ed. (Princeton, N.J.: Princeton University Press, 1990), especially the section entitled "Reasons to Act for a Reason."

one's deliberations in one of those ways, then one is guaranteed normally to succeed in acting acceptably from a moral point of view. Such success requires far more—including, most notably, appropriate moral values and beliefs, good moral judgment, strength of character, sensitivity to the morally relevant features of the circumstances in which one finds oneself, and luck.

It should be clear that even if overtly moral considerations do almost always impinge on one's deliberations in one of the five ways mentioned, the explicit role of such considerations in one's actual thought is bound to be limited. That is because the fifth of the deliberative roles I described, which is surely the role that overtly moral considerations play more frequently than all the others put together, is purely counterfactual. This means that most morally acceptable conduct is prompted by thoughts with no overtly moral content. Nor is this true only, as one might initially suspect, of morally permissible, as opposed to morally required, conduct. The thought with which one does the right thing need not be "this is the right thing to do"; it can just as easily be "he's hungry" or "she didn't mean to" or "that would hurt his feelings" or "I said I'd be there." Thus a morally successful agent will need to be sensitive, not only to overtly moral considerations (moral considerations narrowly understood), but also to considerations like those just mentioned, which lack overtly moral content, but which nevertheless have an important bearing on the moral assessment of what one does (moral considerations broadly understood). What a morally successful agent will certainly not need to do is to engage at all times in the explicit moral assessment of his or her own conduct.

This brings us back to the question of whether, when we formulate a moral assessment of someone else's action, we commit ourselves to any view about what the content of that person's thoughts should be. This should not be confused with the more frequently discussed question of whether such an assessment commits us to any view about what reasons for action the agent has, or about the contents of the agent's existing motivational repertoire.[4] The commitment that is in question here concerns what the agent's delibera-

---

4. This more frequently discussed question, which I do not address, is sometimes represented as a question about the relative merits of *internalism* and *externalism* in ethics. Ethical internalism is not the same as internalism about practical reasons, which does play a role in one or two of my arguments in later chapters. On the distinction between these two forms of internalism, see chapter 8, footnote 2.

tive thoughts should be rather than what his reasons or motives are, and we may begin our response by observing that it would be very odd if our practices of moral assessment committed us to a view about how deliberation should be structured that was incompatible with its actual structure. Although it is perhaps not inconceivable that there should be this kind of misalignment or disorder in our moral thought, I see no reason to believe that such a misalignment exists in fact. If none does, then, in light of what I have said about the variety of ways in which moral considerations impinge on deliberation, and about the variability of people's deliberative styles, it follows that the formulation of a moral assessment does not commit us to any very rigid or specific view of what thoughts the agent should have. It might at most commit us, compatibly with the argument to this point, to thinking that appropriate moral considerations should impinge on the agent's deliberations in one or another of the five ways described. But that would be a very weak commitment, since, as we have seen, it would not wed us to the idea that any overtly moral thought should enter into the agent's actual deliberations at all. Moreover, it would remain a very weak commitment even if, as a possible consequence of our acceptance of the claim of pervasiveness, it were generalized to cover *all* deliberation. For our commitment, thus generalized, would amount to little more than saying that one ought, morally speaking, always to deliberate in such a way that one is led, by more than a mere coincidence, to act acceptably from a moral standpoint. As far as I can see, there is nothing in that thought to legitimate fears of an overmoralized self.

Thus we can formulate a moral assessment of someone's action without implying that any overtly moral thought should enter directly into that person's deliberations. At the same time, however, this does not preclude the possibility that on some occasions we may in fact wish to claim, as an independent matter, that such thoughts should indeed enter directly into the agent's deliberations. It does not even preclude the possibility of claiming that, for acts of certain types, it is a condition of their rightness that overtly moral thoughts of appropriate kinds should enter into the deliberations that precede their performance. To be sure, these claims require interpretation and defense in their own right, if they are to be accepted. For our purposes it suffices to note that, although our use of verdictive moral language does not by itself commit us to making such claims about the acts we are assessing, this does not in turn imply that such claims are always false.

Just as the formulation of an overall moral verdict allows us but does not require us to think that overtly moral thoughts should enter directly into the agent's deliberations, so too it allows us, though it obviously does not require us, to hold, if it seems to us appropriate in the circumstances, that overtly moral thoughts should *not* enter directly into the agent's deliberations, or that it would be undesirable for them to do so. Our reaction to the rescue case we have been discussing, for example, may be that it would be permissible for the man to save his wife, but morally undesirable for him to have the permissibility of so doing as one of his overt deliberative thoughts. There is, so far as I can see, nothing about the formulation of an overall verdict of permissibility that makes it impossible consistently to hold such a view. Thus, not only does the formulation of such a verdict not commit us to thinking that overtly moral thoughts *should* enter directly into the agent's deliberations, it does not even commit us to thinking that it is morally unobjectionable if they happen to do so.[5]

We can now clarify the suggestion that the formulation of an overall moral verdict may at most commit us to the idea that appropriate moral considerations should impinge on the agent's

5. We have already seen that, on one natural reading of Williams's remarks about the rescue case, he is assuming that the stronger of these two commitments obtains, and this is what underlies his allegation that we "provide" the man with "one thought too many," if we say that it would be morally permissible for him to save his wife. On another reading, however, Williams may be interpreted as assuming only that the weaker commitment obtains. That is, he may be interpreted as assuming that, if we regard it as permissible for the man to save his wife, we are committed to claiming, not that the man ought to be motivated in part by the thought of his act's permissibility, but only that it would be unobjectionable if he were so motivated. On this reading, in other words, we "provide" the man with one thought too many, in the sense not that we claim it is a thought he must have, but rather that we view it as a thought he may have. We make it available to him, so to speak. What I am arguing, however, is that the judgment that it would be permissible for the man to save his wife does not commit us even to this weaker claim.

Suppose that the man saves his wife, and that his only thought at the time he does so is that she is his wife. Suppose too that he is subsequently challenged about the justifiability of his action. Although he never actually entertained the thought of his act's permissibility during the rescue episode itself, he responds to the challenge by saying that it is permissible in situations of this kind to save one's wife. Might Williams be assuming only that we are committed, if we regard the man's act as permissible, to claiming that it would be unobjectionable for him to respond to such a challenge in this way? Perhaps, but then Williams's criticism lacks force, since such a commitment, if it obtained, would not be objectionably moralistic.

deliberations in one or another of the five ways described. Such a commitment, if it obtains, is to be understood as permitting but not requiring us, in any given case, to have more specific views about the form that the agent's deliberations should take. In other words, it is compatible with our thinking, in any given situation, either that it would be equally satisfactory for the agent's deliberations to instantiate any one of the five patterns sketched, or that some but not all of those patterns of deliberation would be acceptable, or that only one particular type of deliberation would be appropriate in the circumstances. It is also compatible with our having no opinion at all about this question. In effect, the suggestion is that we may be committed, when we formulate a moral assessment of someone's action, to the idea that moral considerations should impinge on the agent's deliberations in some manner appropriate to the circumstances, but that this leaves us free, on each occasion, either to have or not to have additional views about which particular mode(s) of impingement would in fact be appropriate. If this is correct, then we can formulate a moral assessment of someone's action without holding either that it is mandatory or that it would be unobjectionable for that very assessment to enter directly into the agent's deliberations.

The idea that it is sometimes but not always appropriate for the moral assessment of an action to enter into the agent's own deliberations may appear to invite an objection similar to one often raised against utilitarianism. It is often said that if utilitarianism is to be a plausible view, it cannot insist that people should always be thinking about what would maximize overall utility. Yet, it is claimed, the theory can never consistently allow people fully to turn their attention away from that question, for if they do so they run the risk of missing out on important opportunities to promote the good, and the theory is concerned solely with the promotion of the good. Thus, it is said, whatever else they may be thinking about, utilitarian agents must always be monitoring their circumstances to make sure that no major opportunity of this kind escapes their notice. Similarly, it may seem, if we hold that it is sometimes but not always objectionable for the moral assessment of one's actions to enter into one's deliberations, we must insist that one should always be monitoring one's circumstances so that one knows at each moment whether or not it is appropriate at that moment to be thinking explicitly about the moral legitimacy of what one is doing. But if one is constantly engaged in this kind of monitoring, then one *is* always thinking about the moral legitimacy of one's actions after all.

This objection rests on a failure adequately to distinguish between two different issues. The first is the issue of whether utilitarianism can consistently permit individuals to deliberate about what to do without thinking about what would maximize overall utility, given that the theory sees the maximization of utility as the sole criterion for the rightness of each and every action. No analogue of this issue arises for the view we have been discussing, for that view does not postulate any comparably monistic criterion of right action, or indeed any criterion of right action at all. The second issue may be formulated in terms of a puzzle that might be called the "paradox of nonobsessive thought." Suppose that there is a topic about which it is sometimes but not always appropriate to think. How can one manage to start thinking about that topic precisely when it is appropriate to do so, unless one is already monitoring one's circumstances to see whether the time has come to start thinking about it, in which case one is already thinking about it? This "paradox," however, presents no special difficulty for the view we have been discussing. For it applies to our mental life in general, and its solution is a matter for psychological theory, which must explain (by appealing, for example, to our capacity to recognize cues that alert us to the need to begin thinking about new topics) how we manage to change the focus of our attention in appropriate ways.

Although the two issues just mentioned are distinct, utilitarians sometimes argue that nothing more is required, in order to rebut the criticism of their view raised by the first issue, than to invoke the ordinary mechanisms of attention change whose importance is highlighted by the second issue. By contrast, critics of utilitarianism must explain why they do not believe that those mechanisms suffice to eliminate the objection. Another way in which utilitarians sometimes attempt to rebut such objections is by appealing to the distinction between the utilitarian account of right action and the utilitarian account of optimal deliberation. The right act, it is said, is the one that will maximize overall utility, but the best way for an agent to deliberate need not be by trying to determine which of the options available would achieve such maximization. Instead, the agent should engage in whatever sort of deliberation would itself maximize utility, and this may mean not thinking in explicitly utilitarian terms, or even thinking in explicitly nonutilitarian terms. Indeed, utilitarians sometimes say, agents should not so much as believe in the truth of the utilitarian doctrine, if the effects of such a belief would be nonoptimal. This, in turn, has led critics to charge that utilitarianism violates a requirement of "publicity," which is said to be a condition of the adequacy of any moral outlook. However these issues may be resolved, it should be clear that no comparable objection can be raised to the view I have defended. For I have not argued that it is sometimes morally desirable for people to have false beliefs about the content of morality. I have claimed only that, if we find ourselves independently drawn to the position that it is sometimes inappropriate for the moral assessment of an act to enter into the agent's own deliberations, the language of moral assessment does not prevent us from consistently accepting such a position. In other words, there is no inconsistency in formulating an overall moral verdict about some act, but denying that it would be appropriate for that verdict to enter into the agent's deliberations. Nor, so far as I can see, does such a position violate any plausible requirement of publicity.[6]

Thus in the end I do not think that the moral assessment of action commits us to any view of deliberation that, when combined with the claim of pervasiveness, generates an overmoralized conception of the self. However, the fear of an overmoralized self is a powerful one, and it has had other manifestations in moral philosophy. It has, for instance, found expression in one influential objection to the idea of a "moral theory," where such a theory is understood as a system of general moral principles that can be combined with information about specific circumstances to yield overall moral verdicts about particular actions. Many different objections have been raised to the

6. For further discussion of the issues concerning utilitarianism mentioned in the text, see David Brink, *Moral Realism and the Foundations of Ethics* (Cambridge: Cambridge University Press, 1989), pp. 259–62; Derek Parfit, *Reasons and Persons* (Oxford: Clarendon Press, 1984), chapter 1; Peter Railton, "Alienation, Consequentialism, and the Demands of Morality," *Philosophy and Public Affairs* 13 (1984): 134–71 (rpt. in *Consequentialism and Its Critics,* ed. Samuel Scheffler [Oxford: Oxford University Press, 1988], pp. 93–133); John Rawls, *A Theory of Justice* (Cambridge, Mass.: Harvard University Press, 1971), pp. 177–82; Samuel Scheffler, *The Rejection of Consequentialism* (Oxford: Clarendon Press, 1982), pp. 43–52; Henry Sidgwick, *The Methods of Ethics,* 7th ed. (London: Macmillan, 1907), Book Four; Bernard Williams, "A Critique of Utilitarianism," in *Utilitarianism For and Against,* ed. J. J. C. Smart and Bernard Williams (Cambridge: Cambridge University Press, 1973), pp. 77–150 (rpt. in part in *Consequentialism and Its Critics,* pp. 20–50).

idea of such a theory. Some people, to take just one example, believe that the term 'moral theory' suggests an inappropriate analogy between ethics and science, with moral theories construed, on the model of scientific theories, as testable principles that purport to describe some portion of reality, that can be confirmed or disconfirmed by observational evidence, and so on. Of the people who find this analogy objectionable, some think, in effect, that it gives morality too much credit. By contrast, others object to it because it seems to them symptomatic of an exaggerated devotion to science, which starts by seeing scientific inquiry as the model of intellectual respectability and ends, unsurprisingly, by distorting other areas of inquiry in order to get them to fit the privileged mold. These people think, in effect, that the analogy gives science too much credit. The fear of an overmoralized self is implicated in a different although not unrelated objection. Briefly stated, the objection is that the idea of a moral theory is bound up with an erroneous understanding of the nature of practical reasoning, a tendency to misconceive it as a process of implementing a mechanical decision procedure.[7] However, it is not always clear what precise relationship between the idea of a moral theory and the decision-procedural model of practical reasoning is being alleged. The thought may be something like this: there could be an acceptable moral theory only if human practical reasoning, in its moral dimension at least, either were, or were capable of becoming, just a matter of implementing a mechanical decision procedure; but since neither of these things is in fact true, it follows that there cannot be such a thing as an acceptable moral theory. This skeletal argument clearly requires further development.

Suppose that there were indeed an acceptable moral theory, a system of general principles of moral evaluation that, when combined with the relevant bits of specific information, generated accurate overall moral verdicts about particular actions. Then, it might be argued, there should also be available to individual moral reasoners, in principle at least, a decision procedure for determining what they (or anyone else) morally ought to do. That is, there should be a mechanical sequence of operations, involving the bringing to bear of general principles on specific circumstances, that would

---

7. Such an objection is suggested, for example, by John McDowell in "Virtue and Reason," *The Monist* 62 (1979): 331–50, and by Bernard Williams in the Preface to *Moral Luck* (New York: Cambridge University Press, 1981), pp. ix–xi.

always, if carried out properly, yield the appropriate evaluation. But, the argument might continue, although people do appeal to principle on occasion, nobody consistently reasons as if using such a procedure. That much is clear from the account in this chapter of the diverse ways in which moral considerations impinge on human deliberation. Nor would this situation change if only philosophers could find a better theory, or popularize more effectively one of the ones they already have. Human practical reasoning, it might be said, is deeply resistant to the decision-procedure model; it does not now conform to that model, and there is no imaginable theoretical development that would lead it to.

Even if we suppose—as I will soon deny—that this version of the argument is entirely correct as far as it goes, it is not sufficient to support the conclusion that there can be no such thing as an acceptable moral theory. For that conclusion to be supported along the lines suggested by the original skeletal argument, two things would have to be shown: (1) that there could be an acceptable moral theory only if it were appropriate to think that practical reasoning, in moral contexts at least, is or might actually become just a process of implementing a decision procedure; and (2) that it is not in fact appropriate to think this. While the argument of the preceding paragraph may support (2), it provides no support for (1). Even on the most generous construal, it supports only the weaker claim (1★) that there could be an acceptable moral theory only if there could also be a moral decision procedure that was in principle available to moral reasoners. It does not, in other words, show that the idea of a moral theory commits one to the empirical belief that people actually do or ever would use such a procedure. Nor is it easy to see how this could be shown. So the original skeletal argument may need to be revised.

A revised argument might withdraw claim (1) and supplement claim (1★) with the suggestion that, insofar as human practical decision making, as actually carried out, differs from a process of implementing a decision procedure, any defender of the idea of a moral theory must regard that divergence, if not as eliminable, then at least as regrettable. And those features of moral reasoning and decision that are incongruous with the decision-procedure model must be viewed as unfortunate flaws in our practical apparatus. The decision-procedure model represents an ideal; if we are doomed by our constitutions always to fall short of the ideal, we can only regret it. And yet, the argument might go, it would be perverse to regret it.

To do so would reflect a failure sufficiently to appreciate, a devaluation of, important features of our actual processes of reasoning and decision. Among the features that may be cited are these: the role of sensitivity and perception in picking out the morally salient features of a situation; the role of the imagination in developing the required sensitivity as well as in exercising it; the role of individual judgment in weighing or balancing competing considerations; the difficulty of deciding what the right thing to do is in hard cases; and the ambivalence and regret that are sometimes experienced even when one believes that one is doing the right thing. If the implementation of a decision procedure is thought of as representing some kind of ideal of practical reason, and if human practical reasoning as we actually find it is thought of as a flawed substitute with which we may have to make do, then our attitude toward features such as these must be that we would do away with them if we could. But if, *per impossibile,* they were in fact done away with, and moral reasoning came to consist in the smooth implementation of any imaginable decision procedure whatsoever, the result would be a net loss in both moral and human terms. It would be a net loss in moral terms because such a change would actually lessen our ability accurately to determine what we morally ought to do, by depriving us of tools that are indispensable for that task: tools that no decision procedure could duplicate or replace. It would be a net loss in human terms, both because it would transform an important dimension of individual personality into a matter of skill in mechanical calculation, and because it would vastly expand the place of explicit moral reflection in human deliberation, thereby suggesting a grimly moralistic picture of how such deliberation should be structured.

These last remarks clarify the way in which the fear of an overmoralized self contributes to the objection, and they reveal a parallel with the earlier resistance to the claim of pervasiveness. In each case the thought of moral assessment having some kind of systematic character gives rise to the fear of an overmoralized conception of deliberation. In the earlier case I argued that the fear was unwarranted. It remains to be seen whether it is better founded in this instance.

The revised argument maintains, in effect, that the idea of a moral theory cannot be fully reconciled with a realistic picture of human deliberation, such as the one I tried to sketch at the beginning of this chapter. It claims that someone who accepts the idea of such a theory is committed, perversely, to accepting a decision-procedural model as the ideal of moral deliberation, and to regarding the unattainability of that ideal, if indeed it is unattainable, as cause for real regret. This criticism may be thought of as resting on three independent propositions. The first is that the idea of a moral theory commits one to affirming the in-principle availability of a moral decision procedure. The second is that the idea of a moral theory commits one to thinking that it would be desirable for people to use a moral decision procedure, and to viewing it as regrettable if they are incapable of doing so. And the third proposition is that the idea of a moral theory commits one to thinking that reliance on such a procedure would make it possible to eliminate certain important features of our present deliberative activities. All three of these propositions, it seems to me, are false. If I am right, then the idea of a moral theory as I am understanding it remains fully compatible with a realistic picture of human deliberation.

Consider the third proposition first. Even if the first two propositions were true, this one would still be false. To see this, let us suppose for the moment that anyone who accepted the idea of a moral theory was indeed committed to the in-principle availability of a moral decision procedure, and also to the desirability of people's using such a procedure in their deliberations. What exactly would the commitment to the in-principle availability of a decision procedure involve? It would involve a commitment to saying that, if there were in fact an acceptable moral theory, and if one had full knowledge of its principles, and if one also had full knowledge of the relevant information pertaining to any particular action, and if, further, one perceived each bit of this relevant information *as* relevant, *then* there would also be a mechanical sequence of operations one could perform in order to arrive at an overall moral verdict about the action in question. Suppose, for example, that the theory were some form of utilitarianism and that one had fully mastered its principles. And suppose that one had complete information, with regard to some particular act, about the effects of that act and its alternatives on the utilities of all affected creatures. And suppose, finally, that one were aware of the relevance of all this information. Then there would be a mechanical procedure one could use to determine whether the act was required, forbidden, or whatever. Or suppose instead that the theory were some version of deontology and that one had full knowledge of its principles, including, let us assume, second-order ranking principles to settle any conflicts among first-order principles. And suppose further that one knew everything there was to know about those features of some particular act that were, in the theory's terms, relevant to its rightness or wrongness—that one knew, for example, whether the act violated anyone's rights, fulfilled any pledges or promises, promoted anyone's welfare, betrayed any trusts, infringed anyone's autonomy, and so on. Then, supposing again that one were aware of the relevance of this information, there would be a mechanical procedure one could use to arrive at an overall moral verdict about the act.

If acceptance of the idea of a moral theory committed one to the in-principle availability of a moral decision procedure, then what it would commit one to is something along these lines. But even if it did so commit one, and even if it also committed one to thinking that it would be desirable for people to use such a procedure, it still would not commit one to thinking it either possible or desirable to eliminate the roles played in moral reasoning and decision by the faculties of moral sensitivity, perception, imagination, and judgment. On the contrary, a decision procedure of the kind we have described could not be put into operation without those faculties. For the procedure would be a way of generating an overall verdict, given full information about both theoretical principles and particular morally salient circumstances. And the faculties in question are what give us access to information about such circumstances. So even if the idea of a moral theory committed one to the in-principle availability of a moral decision procedure, and to the in-principle desirability of using it, it still would not commit one to thinking that a smoothly implemented decision procedure could be substituted for the exercise of our actual capacities for moral sensitivity, perception, judgment, and imagination. To be sure, someone who believed that there was an acceptable moral theory might well suggest that one of the functions of the theory was to identify in an abstract and systematic way the saliences we must learn to recognize in practice. But this does not imply that familiarity with the theory would make the capacity for recognition in practice unnecessary.[8]

8. For a related discussion of the complementary roles of moral theorizing and moral perception, see Susan Hurley, *Natural Reasons* (New York: Oxford University Press, 1989), chapter 11, especially section 2. See also Barbara Herman, "The Practice of Moral Judgment," *Journal of Philosophy* 82 (1985): 414–36.

Similarly, even if the first two propositions were true, acceptance of the idea of a moral theory would not commit one to a belief in the eliminability or undesirability of ambivalence and regret in moral contexts. There are at least two reasons why this is so. First, as we have just seen, a moral decision procedure of the kind under discussion would be a way of generating overall moral verdicts, given full information both about theoretical principles and about particular morally salient circumstances. Thus whenever full information was lacking, such a procedure would be necessarily unusable. And of course, whenever such information is lacking, there is ample scope for ambivalence, indecision, regret, and self-doubt, and we are rightly wary of people who are wholly unsusceptible to these feelings. Such wariness is not precluded by the idea of a moral theory, even if we assume that acceptance of that idea does commit one to the in-principle availability of a moral decision procedure, and to the desirability of people's using such a procedure where applicable. Of course anyone might wish that situations of imperfect information obtained less often than they do, so that this source of justified ambivalence and self-doubt might be less prevalent than it is. But someone who accepts the idea of a moral theory is no more committed to, and no less capable of, such a wish than anyone else. Nor, as I have said, is such a person any less capable of preferring that, in the absence of full information, people should be liable to feelings of regret and ambivalence.

Second, it is a conspicuous feature of our actual moral lives that such feelings are not always responses to uncertainty or lack of information, or symptoms of wavering conviction. They are often present even on occasions when we have all the relevant information and are confident that we are doing the right thing.[9] What makes these feelings appropriate, when they are, is the evident fact that one can face situations of moral conflict in which there is no act available that is morally fortunate in every respect. In such situations even the right act may involve pain, or loss, or harm, or dishonor, or costs of some other kind. Given that feelings of ambivalence and regret can be appropriate even when we are confident that we are doing the

---

9. Compare Susan Hurley: "Grounds for regretting an action not done needn't relate to a possibility that the action one in fact did was not what one ought to have done, all things considered. One may have reason for regret even though one is certain that one did what one ought to have done, all things considered" (*Natural Reasons,* p. 172).

right thing, there is nothing in the idea of a moral theory that requires one to be intolerant of such feelings.[10] For even if acceptance of that idea committed one to the in-principle availability of a moral decision procedure, and to the desirability of people's using such a procedure where applicable, that commitment would concern only the procedures for arriving at overall moral verdicts. It would leave

10. Critics have charged that some moral theories cannot make sense of regret in these contexts, because they cannot make sense of the idea of genuine moral conflict to begin with. Thus, in a well-known passage from his paper "Ethical Consistency" (included in his *Problems of the Self* [Cambridge: Cambridge University Press, 1973], pp. 166–86), Bernard Williams argues that it is "a fundamental criticism of many ethical theories that their accounts of moral conflict and its resolution do not do justice to the facts of regret and related considerations: basically because they eliminate from the scene the *ought* not acted upon" (p. 175). Such charges are most plausible when directed against "monistic" theories, which regard all moral values as reducible to a single value. However, there is nothing in the idea of a moral theory that excludes pluralism about values, and such charges have little force when directed against theories which recognize a plurality of heterogeneous values, but which hold that, when conflicts of value do arise, there may nevertheless be an answer to the question of what one is required, all things considered, to do. (In this connection, see Hurley, *Natural Reasons,* chapters 7–13, and especially pp. 125–35, 171–75, and 256–64.) We might say that such theories seek to *resolve* conflicts, but not to *eliminate* them. On this use of terminology, it would be a mistake to suggest, as Williams does in "Conflicts of Values" (included in *Moral Luck,* pp. 71–82), that moral theories arise out of a perceived "need to eliminate conflict" (p. 81).

In recent years there has been considerable debate about the nature of moral conflicts, prompted largely by the suggestions of some philosophers, including Williams, Bas van Fraassen, and Philippa Foot, among others, that some moral conflicts may be not only ineliminable but also irresolvable. I do not consider these suggestions here, since the compatibility of regret with the idea of a moral theory can be established without doing so. (See Bas van Fraassen, "Values and the Heart's Command," *Journal of Philosophy* 70 [1973]: 5–19, and Philippa Foot, "Moral Realism and Moral Dilemma," *Journal of Philosophy* 80 [1983]: 379–98. Williams's most notable writings about the nature of moral conflicts include, in addition to the papers already cited, "Consistency and Realism" [in *Problems of the Self,* pp. 187–206], "Moral Luck" [in *Moral Luck,* pp. 20–39], and "Politics and Moral Character" [in *Moral Luck,* pp. 54–70]. See also Ruth Marcus, "Moral Dilemmas and Consistency," *Journal of Philosophy* 77 [1980]: 121–36; Thomas Nagel, "War and Massacre," in *Mortal Questions* [Cambridge: Cambridge University Press, 1979], pp. 53–74, and "The Fragmentation of Value," in *Mortal Questions,* pp. 128–41. A number of the most influential of the recent papers on moral conflict, including those by van Fraassen, Marcus, and Foot, and also Williams's "Ethical Consistency" and Nagel's "The Fragmentation of Value," have been included in *Moral Dilemmas,* ed. Christopher Gowans [New York: Oxford University Press, 1987].)

Williams has suggested that some moral theorists try, misguidedly, to accommodate regret by construing it as a nonmoral feeling. (See "Ethical Consistency," section 5, and *Ethics and the Limits of Philosophy* [Cambridge, Mass.: Harvard University Press, 1985], pp. 176–77. See also van Fraassen, "Values and the Heart's Command," section 5.) It should be clear that, in arguing that regret is compatible with the idea of a moral theory, I am not relying on any such construal.

the facts about what feelings are compatible with such verdicts untouched. Thus the third proposition would be false even if the first two were true.

Consider the second proposition next. And suppose again that the first proposition were true: that the idea of a moral theory did commit one to the in-principle availability of a moral decision procedure. It might then be suggested that, although the falsity of the third proposition means that the idea of a moral theory does not commit one to thinking that it would be desirable for people to use a decision procedure for moral reasoning *instead of* exercising their capacities for moral sensitivity, judgment, perception, and the like, it does nevertheless commit one to thinking that it would be desirable for them to use such a procedure, albeit in conjunction with the capacities mentioned. If this suggestion were true, it would need to be explained why such a commitment was objectionable, since the original reason for finding a commitment to the desirability of a decision procedure objectionable was the thought that it implied a devaluation of our actual moral faculties—a thought that has now been discredited. But the suggestion is false in any case. As we have seen, a commitment to the in-principle availability of a moral decision procedure is a commitment to saying that, if one had full knowledge of the relevant moral principles, and if one also had full knowledge of the relevant information pertaining to any particular action, and if, further, one perceived each bit of this relevant information *as* relevant, then there would be a mechanical sequence of procedures one could perform in order to arrive at an overall moral assessment of the action in question. It involves no additional commitment to saying that, in the hypothetical case where all these conditions were met, it would automatically be desirable to use this mechanical sequence of procedures if one wanted to obtain the moral assessment. For, from the mere availability of a decision procedure, it hardly follows that one ought to use it. In general, a decision procedure may be cumbersome, inefficient, time-consuming, or in other ways ill suited to the circumstances. Other processes or heuristic strategies may have decisive advantages, and there is nothing in the idea of a moral theory to prevent one from acknowledging this.[11] Thus there is, for example, no reason why acceptance

---

11. As we have seen, some utilitarians go much further and argue that their theory actually implies that, under certain conditions, people should not even accept the truth

of that idea would commit one to thinking that it would be preferable if people's deliberations did not exhibit the kind of diversity sketched at the beginning of this chapter.

It is worth saying what should be obvious, and what that diversity itself suggests, namely, that questions about the preferred place of moral principles in our thoughts and practices do not admit only of the two extreme answers represented by the idea of a decision procedure on the one hand, and by a particularism that denies them any role on the other.[12] In the territory between these extremes, three things seem to me worthy of special attention. One is the role of such principles in helping to shape our social and political institutions, educational practices, and processes of acculturation, and through them the moral sensibilities that enable us to decide many moral questions without any explicit appeal to principle. The second is our tendency to treat principles as resources in cases in which we are uncertain and feel ourselves in need of moral guidance. And the third is the role of explicit appeals to principle in our attempts to explain and justify our beliefs and behavior, both to ourselves and to others, and the consequent prominence of such appeals in social and political argument and debate. The full story of how moral principles do and should enter into our individual reflections and social practices is a complicated one, and there is nothing in the idea of a moral theory that must blind us to this complexity, or lead us to think that a simpler state of affairs would be preferable. The second proposition is false.

And so, too, in the end, is the first proposition: the idea of a moral theory does not even commit one to the in-principle availability of a moral decision procedure. Recall that such a procedure, if there were one, would be a routine method capable of yielding a determinate overall moral verdict about any action, given full information about both general principles and particular circumstances.[13] But someone

---

of the theory itself, let alone attempt always to deliberate exclusively in its terms. The points made in the text remain true, whatever the merits of this particular utilitarian argument.

12. See Jonathan Dancy, "Ethical Particularism and Morally Relevant Properties," *Mind* 92 (1983): 530–47.

13. Compare S. C. Kleene:

We know examples in mathematics of general questions, such that any particular instance of the question can be answered by a preassigned uniform method.

can accept the idea of a moral theory, understood as a system of general principles for the moral evaluation of action, without believing that there must be a determinate overall verdict for every single act,[14] let alone that there is a mechanical routine guaranteed in every instance to lead us to it. Only with the aid of strong auxiliary assumptions will one get from the idea that there exists a system of evaluative principles to the idea that those principles are powerful enough to generate a determinate evaluation for every single act. Of course certain particular theories and theorists do in fact make the latter claim. Others do not, however, and the idea of a moral theory does not itself require it.[15]

Two rather different objections may be raised at this point. The first is that it is misleading to use the term 'theory' if all one has in mind is a system of evaluative principles that may or may not be capable of generating a determinate answer in every case. The second is that the original criticism was meant to link the idea of a moral theory not to a decision procedure in the technical sense of the term, but rather to a less strict but still objectionable idea about how

---

> More precisely, in such an example, there is an infinite class of particular questions, and a procedure in relation to that class, both being described in advance, such that if we thereafter select any particular question of the class, the procedure will surely apply and lead us to a definite answer, either "yes" or "no", to the particular question selected. . . . A method of this sort . . . we will call a decision procedure. (*Introduction to Metamathematics* [New York: Van Nostrand, 1952], p. 136)

14. The possibility I am imagining should be distinguished from two others. It is not the same as the idea that there may be situations in which there is no morally permissible course of action open to the agent, so that anything he or she does will be wrong. Nor is it the same as the idea that morality is not pervasive—that some acts are simply ineligible for moral assessment. The possibility I am envisioning is that an assessment of a given set of options may reveal it to have features that make it impossible for a particular moral theory to give any guidance about which option to choose. The resources of the theory—and, if we accept the theory, of morality itself—are baffled by the circumstances. Someone might insist that it is impossible for morality to be baffled by any set of circumstances, so that any theory that was would have to be wrong. Perhaps this is so, but it is something that would have to emerge from a more general account of the kind of thing morality is; it does not follow from the very idea of a moral theory.

15. Thus, for example, John Rawls writes that "not all the moral questions we are prompted to ask in everyday life have answers. Indeed, perhaps only a few of them can be settled by any moral conception that we can understand and apply" ("Kantian Constructivism in Moral Theory: The Dewey Lectures 1980," *Journal of Philosophy* 77 [1980]: 563).

moral decisions do and should get made. Thus, in effect, the interpretation against which I have been arguing is a red herring.

The term 'theory' stands at the center of many philosophical controversies and has many different sorts of association. Thus I agree, in response to the first objection, that the use of that term to refer to systems of substantive moral principles, whose precise character and status are matters of intense controversy, can be misleading if not clearly explained. However, it is by now common practice to use the term in this way. And certainly the meaning of 'theory' is sufficiently elastic that no linguistic error is involved. Provided that the intended usage is made clear, therefore, I do not believe that any serious harm is done. The second objection, meanwhile, is unpersuasive, because the original criticism derives its apparent force precisely from the technical associations of the term 'decision procedure'. If the criticism was never meant to invoke those associations, it is hard to see why the term was used in the first place. And if there is a red herring swimming in these waters, the likeliest candidate is the original criticism itself. In any event, it is unclear how that criticism is to be understood, if it is not construed as invoking the technical notion of a decision procedure. Perhaps the claim is simply that the idea of a moral theory implies that general principles have some role to play in practical deliberation. If so, I doubt whether the claim is correct, and even if it is, it hardly counts as an objection, since principles do have some role to play in practical deliberation.

Thus the fear of an overmoralized self is unwarranted as a response to the idea of a moral theory, for the claim that that idea is objectionably connected with a decision-procedural model of moral reasoning is not true. Nevertheless, it must be conceded that that claim and others like it may to some extent be encouraged by a picture of morality that has considerable currency in contemporary philosophy, and that makes heavy use of the concept of a moral theory. According to this picture, morality consists in a set of principles or propositions. Moral theories are also systems of propositions, and each theory purports correctly to capture the content of morality itself. Everyone subscribes, consciously or unconsciously, to some moral theory, however commonsensical or unsophisticated, and does so on some grounds or other. People use their theories to determine what they ought to do. Different people, of course, subscribe to different theories, and some theories are better than others. Fundamental moral disagreements are disagreements about which theory is best. Through argument, a rational person can be led to adopt a superior theory. Moral change and moral development consist in adopting new theories to replace old ones, preferably on the basis of rational considerations.

Critics of this picture argue that morality does not fundamentally consist in a set of principles or propositions, and that most people have never "adopted" any "moral theory." A fortiori, most people do not use such theories to make decisions. Morality, insofar as it is something real and not a philosopher's fiction, is an aspect of human psychology and social relations, and not a system of propositions. Its development within an individual is part of that individual's psychohistory. It gets entrenched in human beings and comes to have an important role to play in their lives, not by virtue of being adopted on the strength of convincing arguments, but rather by answering to powerful psychological needs, engaging basic human emotions, and serving significant social and psychological functions. And however real moral change may occur, it is not as a result of being persuaded to adopt a new theory.

Interestingly, this line of criticism involves an assumption that appears tacitly to be accepted by the very picture it is directed against: namely, that there is of necessity an opposition between thinking of morality in terms of sets of propositions, or theories, and thinking of it as a feature of human psychologies.[16] By contrast, I assume that these are two complementary forms of understanding: that an interest in the propositions of morality does not commit one to believing in a morality of disembodied propositions. Accordingly, although I agree that the picture I have described involves significant distortion and exaggeration, I do not believe that recognition of this fact requires us to give up the idea of a moral theory altogether.

---

16. Compare Richard Wollheim:

> There are two very broad ways of thinking about morality—each suggests how morality should be primarily thought of, and how it should be thought of derivatively—and which of these two broad ways we subscribe to will condition what we expect of morality and what we allow it to expect of us.
> On one view, morality is thought of primarily as a set of thoughts or propositions. . . . On the other view, morality is thought of primarily as a part of the psychology of the person, or of how we live, including in its domain certain beliefs and emotions, certain thoughts and feelings, and a number of habits. (*The Thread of Life* [Cambridge, Mass.: Harvard University Press, 1984], pp. 197–98)

However, if moral theories are not thought of as functioning in the manner suggested by the picture, and if they are not thought of as aiming to provide us with a moral decision procedure, it may be wondered what exactly the point or function of such theories is. Needless to say, people with different views about the metaphysical and epistemological status of ethics may ultimately give different answers to this question.[17] However, even without a metaethical consensus, I think we can say enough to reassure ourselves that moral theories can serve a legitimate and indeed important function. For whatever else they may be, moral theories embody competing proposals about the types of features that are morally salient, and about the nature of the priority relations among different types of salient features. In other words, each theory constitutes an abstract representation of a scheme of moral salience. Some theories aim to match our existing patterns of moral response as closely as possible, while others offer substantial challenges to well-entrenched habits of moral thought. In formulating and arguing about these theories, philosophers engage in a form of reflective activity that is continuous with the moral and intellectual life of the culture as a whole. Debates about the salience of different types of features, about the relative importance of different types of salient features, and about whether existing patterns of moral response should be altered or preserved, are central concerns of the culture itself. This is obviously not to say that there is no need for philosophers to try to understand the nature of moral truth, moral objectivity, and moral knowledge, and thereby to deepen our understanding of the status of the rival schemes of salience embodied in competing moral theories. Nor is it to say that philosophers can afford to argue about such schemes without worrying about what counts as a good argument or why. It is simply to say that, in the absence of anything approaching a consensus about these matters, we need not fear that only a mis-guided philosophical account of human deliberation and individual psychology could lead us to think such schemes of salience worth formulating and arguing about. On the contrary, in this area philosophers take on an imperative that is felt by the culture as a whole: to formulate, to compare, to criticize, to reflect, and to wonder about the possibilities of change, both for the better and for the worse.

17. Two sophisticated recent proposals are those of Susan Hurley in *Natural Reasons* (especially Part III), and T. M. Scanlon in "The Aims and Authority of Moral Theory," *Oxford Journal of Legal Studies* (forthcoming).

FOUR

Overridingness, Human Correctness, and Motivational Naturalism

As I have indicated, I wish to defend a view of morality as pervasive but moderate. As noted in chapter 2, this leaves open the question whether morality is overriding. I have serious doubts about the claim of overridingness, and in the course of this chapter I will indicate in general terms what they are. I also believe, however, that many of the arguments typically offered against the claim are inconclusive. Moreover, such arguments are often inspired by conceptions of moral motivation that are themselves open to criticism. Thus before pursuing any doubts of my own about the claim, I want to explain why so much of what is said in opposition to it is unconvincing.

Since different people mean different things when they talk about the overridingness of morality, it is worth repeating that what I call the "claim of overridingness," or "CO" for short, is the claim that it can never be rational knowingly to do what morality forbids. So understood, CO is a claim about the rationality of actions, not of people. If on some occasion one does knowingly do what morality forbids, CO does not imply that one is an irrational person, only that one has not on this occasion acted in a rational way. How is the term 'rational' being used here? In some contexts, to describe an action as rational is simply to say that it is motivated by some reason and explainable by reference to that reason. Clearly, however, CO is not the claim that immoral acts are never motivated or explainable by reasons. Alternatively, 'rational' may be used in an explicitly normative way. In this spirit, rational action is sometimes by definition taken to be action that best promotes the agent's interests, or instead, that best satisfies the agent's existing desires. As it occurs in the formulation of CO that I have given, 'rational' is indeed used normatively, but it is to be understood as meaning simply 'optimal from the standpoint of reason'.[1] Given this usage, the assertion that the rational action is the one that most effectively promotes the agent's interests is to be regarded as a substantive claim rather than as a definitional truth. So too the assertion that practical rationality consists in maximizing the satisfaction of the agent's existing desires. These two different claims may be referred to as the *prudential* and *instrumental* conceptions of rationality, respectively. On my use of the term 'rational', neither conception is true by definition. Thus although, as we shall soon see, some have tried to defend CO by embracing the prudential conception and attempting to show that morality and self-interest always coincide,[2] the occurrence of the term 'rational' in the formulation I have given does not make this, by definition, the only possible way to defend that thesis. Indeed, I will soon suggest that this type of defense in fact constitutes a rather special case.

First, however, there is one additional point to be made about the formulation of CO that I have given. Normative judgments of rationality or irrationality are often understood as relative to the information available to the agent. That is why I have construed CO as the claim that it can never be rational *knowingly* to do what morality forbids. So construed, CO allows that an agent who was unaware that an act was wrong might act rationally in performing it. Another way of putting this point would be to say that such an agent might act rationally in doing the wrong thing, even though it was not what he or she had *most reason to do,* where judgments about what one has reason to do are regarded as less dependent on the information one has. Accordingly, some people may prefer to formulate CO itself as the claim that doing what morality forbids can never be what one has most reason to do. I will continue to use the original

1. In this usage, correspondingly, 'irrational' means 'nonoptimal from the standpoint of reason'.

2. It would, of course, be logically possible to construct a parallel defense of CO by appealing to the instrumental conception and then arguing that adherence to moral norms always maximizes the satisfaction of the agent's existing desires. However, few people would regard this as a plausible way to defend CO. As we shall see, CO's incompatibility with the instrumental conception as I have defined it is less controversial than its incompatibility with the prudential conception.

formulation most of the time, but nothing of substance turns on it, and I will treat the two formulations as interchangeable.

It is important to distinguish at the outset among four different positions, all of which accept CO. The first two regard CO as true because they believe that it is rational to do what will maximally advance one's own interests, and because they believe that the dictates of morality and self-interest are conceptually guaranteed never to conflict. The first position secures this conceptual guarantee by defining morality in terms of the agent's interests, while the second position secures it by defining the agent's interests in terms of the moral life.[3] The third position agrees that it is rational to do what will maximally advance one's own interests, but does not claim that morality and self-interest are conceptually guaranteed never to conflict. Instead, it maintains that, as a matter of fact, adherence to (independently characterized) moral norms always serves the interests of the agent. This position thus agrees with the previous two in asserting that morality and self-interest never conflict, but it sees this as a happy empirical circumstance rather than as a conceptual truth. The fourth position, meanwhile, denies that practical rationality consists solely in the maximization of self-interest, and holds that it is never rational knowingly to do what morality forbids, even though the demands of morality may indeed conflict with the agent's own interests. There is thus a fundamental difference between the first three positions, all of which accept the prudential conception of rationality and deny that conflicts between morality and self-interest ever occur, and the fourth position, which rejects the prudential conception and affirms the existence of such conflicts. Now the very term 'overriding' suggests the possibility of conflict. Thus although all four positions accept the claim of overridingness as I have defined it, the first three are in a sense special cases. For their acceptance of CO depends on the view that morality and self-interest never conflict, and that view, although important, is most naturally considered independently of the question of overridingness. Accordingly, I will take up that view, which I believe to be mistaken, in

---

3. Thomas Nagel discusses these two positions in *The View From Nowhere* (New York: Oxford University Press, 1986), chapter 10. He identifies five possible views, of which these are the first two, concerning the relation between what he calls "the good life" and "the moral life." He rejects these first two views, and says that the hard choice is between his fourth position, which is that the moral life overrides the good life, and his fifth position, which is that neither consistently overrides the other.

chapter 7, while in this chapter and the next I will focus exclusively on the fourth position. That is, I will simply assume in these two chapters that conflicts between morality and self-interest do arise, and that any adequate defense of CO will have to show that it is true despite the existence of such conflicts. This means that any adequate defense will have to show, among other things, that the prudential conception of rationality is false.

To avoid confusion, it is necessary to distinguish CO from some related but nevertheless independent kinds of assertion. First, we may note that there are typically a number of factors bearing on the question of what one morally ought to do in a given situation, and that if there is a consideration supporting the conclusion that one ought to do A, but a weightier consideration supporting the conclusion that one ought to do B, then it is natural to speak of the second consideration as overriding the first. This is a matter of one consideration overriding another in determining what the overall moral verdict on a given act is, and as such it is clearly independent of CO, which is the claim that it can never be rational knowingly to act contrary to an overall moral verdict.

Second, we may further note that, in the determination of overall moral verdicts, two specific kinds of cases are especially relevant to this discussion: cases in which considerations of cost to the agent override other considerations, and cases in which considerations of cost to the agent are overridden by other considerations. As I said in chapter 2, those who believe that morality is stringent see cases of the first kind as arising less often, and cases of the second kind as arising more often, than do those who believe that morality is moderate, so that stringency may be thought of as the relatively frequent overriding of the agent's interests in arriving at overall moral verdicts. However, as I also said in chapter 2, this does not mean that CO is equivalent to the claim that morality is stringent. CO is a claim about the rationality of defying overall moral verdicts, not a claim about which factors are weightiest in determining the content of such verdicts.

Finally, we should observe that it is sometimes said of certain people that they *treat moral considerations as overriding,* in the sense that they do not knowingly do what morality forbids. As should be evident from the discussion in chapter 3, the treating of moral considerations as overriding, understood in this way, is a highly complex deliberative phenomenon. For present purposes, however, the important point is that the assertion that a particular person treats moral considerations as overriding is independent of CO. For what CO claims is not that some people do in fact treat moral considerations as overriding, but rather that nobody can ever rationally fail to do so.[4]

CO is a very strong claim. Just because it is so strong, it seems to me unlikely to be true. Nevertheless, it is an interesting fact that many of the arguments actually offered against CO are quite inconclusive.[5] Such arguments often take the following form. They first describe a hypothetical situation in which an agent must choose between two courses of action. One of these would satisfy something that sounds like a paradigmatically moral desideratum: it would involve keeping a promise, say, or respecting a right. However, this course of action would also be very problematic in some way for the agent: either it would adversely affect his interests or the interests of someone he cares greatly about, or it would thwart some important goal or aim or purpose of his, or it would be incompatible with some code or style of conduct to which he is committed. The other course of action has the opposite characteristics; it would neither satisfy the moral desideratum nor be personally problematic for the agent. It is then presumed, in such arguments, that the overall moral verdict is that the agent ought to choose the first course of action. At the same time, we are invited to agree that what might be called the "humanly correct" thing to do in this situation is to choose the second course of action. From this it follows that morality gives the "humanly incorrect" answer in such cases, and since it can hardly be irrational to do what is humanly correct, it seems that in these cases it is not irrational to do what morality forbids. Hence CO is false.

---

4. By contrast, R. M. Hare, in *Moral Thinking* (Oxford: Clarendon Press, 1981), identifies overridingness as a "logical property of moral language" (p. 24); but what he means by this is that, in addition to being universal and prescriptive, a principle must, if it is to be numbered among a person's moral principles, either be treated by the person as overriding, or be suitably related to some principle that is so treated (see pp. 50–61).

5. Arguments against overridingness, some but not all of which follow the pattern described in the text, may be found in two papers by Philippa Foot, "Morality as a System of Hypothetical Imperatives" and "Are Moral Considerations Overriding?," in *Virtues and Vices,* pp. 157–73 and 181–88, respectively; in Michael Slote, *Goods and Virtues* (Oxford: Clarendon Press, 1983), chapter 4; and, along with arguments against stringency and pervasiveness, from which they are not always clearly distinguished, in the writings of Bernard Williams and Susan Wolf.

Some such arguments are unconvincing because they fail to make a persuasive case for the human correctness of the course of action they wish to defend, the course of action that fails to satisfy the moral desideratum. When they *are* persuasive on this score, however, the important question is whether they are also correct in supposing it morally required, in the circumstances described, to choose the humanly incorrect option. It may seem that they are. For it may seem that, in each of the relevant examples, there are moral considerations that favor the humanly incorrect course of action, but none that support the humanly correct alternative. And if one assumes, as seems plausible, that overall moral verdicts can be based only on moral considerations, it appears to follow that, in these examples, the humanly incorrect course of action is morally required.

This line of reasoning owes its apparent plausibility to the multiple ambiguity of the term 'moral consideration', which has been responsible for a great deal of confusion in discussions of overridingness.[6] Although that term can be understood in various ways, there is no one way of understanding it that makes plausible both the claim that all the moral considerations in these cases favor the humanly incorrect option, and the claim that overall moral verdicts can be based only on moral considerations.

Consider three different ways in which the line of reasoning may be interpreted, corresponding to three different ways of understanding the term 'moral consideration'. The first interpretation involves what I referred to in chapter 3 as a "narrow" use of that term. On this interpretation, the claim that all of the moral considerations support the humanly incorrect option amounts to the claim that all of the considerations *cast in explicitly moral terms* support that option. However, while this claim may perhaps be true, the line of reasoning we are examining is clearly doomed, if the notion of a moral consideration is understood in this way. For, as we saw in chapter 3, it is clearly not the case that overall moral verdicts can be based only on considerations cast in overtly or explicitly moral terms.

On the second interpretation, the notion of a moral consideration that is employed is not the notion of an overtly or explicitly moral consideration, but rather the notion of a consideration that has *paradigmatic moral relevance*. The consideration that an act would

6. The fact that it is sometimes unclear whether the term is being used to refer to verdictive or evidential considerations is noted by Foot in pp. 181–84 of "Are Moral Considerations Overriding?"

violate someone's rights, which is indeed cast in explicitly moral terms, certainly counts as a moral consideration on this usage, but so does the consideration that an act would cause someone's death, which is not. On the other hand, considerations about the effects of a candidate action on the agent's interests and purposes are assumed not to have paradigmatic moral relevance, and hence not to be moral considerations in this sense. Now once moral considerations are understood in this way, it may again turn out to be true that, in the cases under discussion, there are moral considerations that favor the humanly incorrect option and none that favor the humanly correct alternative. However, the claim that overall moral verdicts can be based only on considerations of this kind, and that the agent's interests and purposes count for nothing, morally speaking, is highly implausible. Considerations of cost to the agent have at least some moral relevance on almost any view. As we have already seen, even those who regard morality as stringent standardly accept this point. Thus to deny it is, in effect, to embrace the claim of stringency in an unusually extreme and implausible form. Since the second version of the line of reasoning we are considering does precisely this, it too fails to show that morality and human correctness diverge in the examples under discussion.

The third interpretation involves what I referred to in chapter 3 as the "broad" use of 'moral consideration', according to which any consideration that supports an overall moral verdict counts as a moral consideration, whether or not it is cast in explicitly moral terms, and whether or not it has paradigmatic moral relevance. Given this usage, the claim that overall moral verdicts can be based only on moral considerations is tautologically true. Obviously enough, however, the problem with this interpretation is that no reason whatsoever has been provided for thinking that all the moral considerations broadly construed favor the humanly incorrect course of action in the relevant examples.

Thus on none of the three interpretations does the line of reasoning we have been considering succeed in demonstrating that morality and human correctness diverge in the examples to which the arguments against CO appeal. In the absence of a convincing demonstration, those arguments are inconclusive, for the idea that morality requires humanly incorrect behavior in the relevant cases will seem plausible only if one regards morality as very demanding. And that is just to say that it will seem plausible only if one accepts the claim of stringency, although not necessarily in its extreme form. Even in its less extreme form, however, the claim of stringency is controversial; it cannot be simply taken for granted. And those who regard morality as moderate have available to them an alternative understanding of the examples on which the arguments against CO rest: namely, that it is morally acceptable in such cases to do the humanly correct thing. If this diagnosis is accepted, then those examples have no force against CO.[7] Indeed, if morality is thought of as moderate, it becomes very hard to think of any case in which it is clear that one course of action is humanly correct but that something else is morally required. In a sense, the question whether morality is moderate or stringent can be viewed as equivalent to the question whether it is the business of morality to be humanly correct. This does not mean that the moderate position sees morality as always coinciding with self-interest, for the concept of "humanly

---

7. It is interesting to compare Foot's diagnosis of what she regards as the deceptive plausibility of CO:

> One may wonder why the proposition that moral considerations are overriding considerations has received so much support. What is it that makes the thought so persuasive? This is, I think, quite easy to explain. Let us go back to the contrast between morality and etiquette, which seems to be what most people have in mind when they argue that moral considerations are overriding. The fact is that there *is* a difference between the way the two codes are taught which is of just the right kind to explain why morality is supposed to be overriding in some significant way.
> . . . Etiquette, unlike morality, is taught as a rigid set of rules that are on occasion to be broken. We do not, as we might have done, incorporate the exceptions to rules about handshaking and so on into the code of etiquette. . . . But morality we teach differently. Moral rules are not taught as rigid rules that it is sometimes right to ignore; rather we teach that it is sometimes *morally permissible* to tell lies (social lies), break promises (as e.g. when ill on the day of an appointment) and refuse help (when the cost of giving it would be, as we say, disproportionate). So we tend, in our teaching, to accommodate the exceptions *within* morality, and with this flexibility it is not surprising that morality can seem "unconditional" and "absolute." In the official code of behaviour morality appears as strong because it takes care never to be on the losing side. ("Are Moral Considerations Overriding?," pp. 186–87)

What Foot says here does not seem very far from what would be expressed in the terminology I have introduced by asserting that morality's tendency to be "humanly correct" makes the claim that it is overriding seem plausible. However, her last sentence is puzzling. It sounds like a complaint, as if there were something suspicious about this feature of morality. After all, we rightly mistrust *people* who take care never to be on the losing side. But why should its human correctness be grounds for a complaint about morality? Perhaps the idea is that morality deliberately contrives to be humanly correct as a way of tricking us into thinking that it is overriding. But what could this even mean?

correct" action, as I am understanding it, is not coextensive with the concept of self-interested action; there are times when the "humanly correct" thing is to do what is morally required at some net cost to oneself. What it does mean is that cases in which it seems to us humanly insupportable to be guided by some paradigmatically "moral" consideration count against CO only if one assumes that morality requires humanly insupportable conduct: an assumption that is not innocuous, and whose denial does not depend on a conviction that morality and self-interest always coincide.

In short, many arguments against CO are inconclusive because they tacitly depend on the supposition that morality is stringent, for which they typically do not argue. This does not imply, however, that anyone who denies that morality is overriding must regard it as stringent. The point of this discussion has been to show that certain influential arguments against overridingness have force only on the assumption that morality is stringent. What follows from this, for those who believe that morality is neither stringent nor overriding, is simply that they must have some other reason for rejecting CO. My own view, as I have said, is that CO is such a strong claim that it is unlikely to be true, even if morality is thought of as moderate rather than stringent, and despite the difficulty in providing conclusive arguments against the claim.

Before elaborating on this view, however, I want to discuss another reason for dissatisfaction with the usual sorts of opposition to CO. Not only do many of the arguments against the claim rely on the unsupported assumption that morality is stringent, but in addition, objections to it often derive their inspiration from a problematic conception of moral motivation whose roots lie in the account provided by Hume. As he is ordinarily interpreted, Hume holds that, in general, only sentiments or desires are ultimately capable of moving a person to action. Reasoning may enable us to determine the most effective ways of attaining our ends, and in so doing may make us aware of considerations that can motivate us, given our ends, but those ends themselves are fixed by our sentiments or desires, which constitute the ultimate source of our motivations for acting. Hume believes that this general view of human motivation applies to the moral case as well as any other. Thus, on his view, any motivations that people may have to behave morally must also derive ultimately from their desires or sentiments. Now when Hume's general motivational view, or a sufficiently similar position, is combined with the *internalist* principle that nothing can count as a reason for a person to act in a certain way unless it is capable of actually motivating him to do so, what follows is a form of the instrumental conception of practical rationality. According to the instrumental conception, any reason that an agent has to act in one way rather than another must derive ultimately from the agent's existing desires. And what it is rational for an agent to do on any given occasion is whatever will best satisfy those desires. As applied to the moral case in particular, the instrumental conception implies that, insofar as agents have reasons to do what morality demands of them, those reasons too must derive ultimately from their existing desires. And of course, it will be rational for an agent to do what morality demands on a given occasion just in case that is what will best satisfy his or her desires. In order for CO to be true, given these views, it would have to be the case that the existing desires of every agent would, on every occasion, best be satisfied by morally acceptable conduct. But this seems like a staggeringly implausible empirical supposition.[8] So, given these views, CO is almost certainly false.

This line of argument has been very influential. Some suitably modified version of it may even be correct. However, there are a number of serious objections to all the most familiar variants of the conception of moral motivation on which this formulation of the argument rests. I will spend the remainder of this chapter examining some of these objections, beginning with a fundamental criticism that was given its most powerful expression by Kant. One of the great themes of the *Foundations of the Metaphysics of Morals* is the incompatibility of our own prephilosophical understanding of morality with any purely naturalistic account of moral motivation: that is, with the idea that our motivations for behaving morally stem ultimately from our natural attitudes, desires, sentiments, or inclinations, or from other features of our psychology. Kant believes that, rightly or wrongly, we ascribe to morality a special kind of motivational authority—a kind of authority that could not possibly have a purely naturalistic source.

8. We noted earlier that some have tried to defend CO by identifying practical rationality with the maximization of self-interest and arguing that morality and self-interest always coincide. By contrast, few if any have attempted to defend CO by advancing an instrumental conception of rationality and arguing that adherence to moral norms always maximizes the satisfaction of the agent's existing desires. CO's incompatibility with an instrumental conception of rationality is less controversial than its incompatibility with a prudential conception.

As Kant sees it, the motivation that we think of as distinctively moral is motivation by a sense of duty. And motivation by a sense of duty is a peculiar kind of motivation, which we sharply distinguish from motivation by sentiment, however other-directed the sentiment may be. Motivation by a sense of duty neither derives from nor depends on the presence of a feeling or sentiment, and it can move us to action even in the absence of any prior inclination to do the right thing. When one is motivated by a sense of duty, one is responsive to the authority of reason rather than to the urgings of one's natural inclinations; one acts as one does because one sees that there are good reasons to do so, and whether or not one happens also to feel like it. Although it may often happen that people do the right thing out of sentiment or inclination, and although their motives on such occasions may have admirable features, nevertheless these motives do not count for us as distinctively moral, and the actions they motivate do not exhibit the special form of praiseworthiness that constitutes moral praiseworthiness.

Kant thinks that this is our own implicit prephilosophical view of the matter, our common understanding, as revealed by our patterns of moral thought and judgment and our practices of moral comment and assessment. For example, Kant says that the commands of morality as we ordinarily think of them are not conditional on the presence in the agent of any particular sentiment or sentiments. We do not regard morality as telling us how to treat people if, say, we happen to like them or feel sympathetically disposed toward them. Rather, we regard it as setting limits to the ways in which we can treat individuals even if we do not like them, or sympathize with them, or for that matter know them. This suggests that, for us, to be motivated morally—by morality—is to be motivated by a conception of the treatment that one owes to people as people, however one happens to feel about them, rather than by some feeling or sentiment or inclination. And in fact, Kant thinks, this suggestion is confirmed by looking at the cases in which we judge people's actions to display moral worth. On the one hand, he argues, personal warmth and affection, for all their human importance, are not in themselves the kinds of motives that we think of as distinctively moral, and so we tend not to assign moral worth to acts when we believe that such sentiments alone are prompting them, and that a sense of duty is playing no motivational role. On the other hand, we are prepared to classify an act we take to be performed out of duty as morally worthy, even if we think that a sense of duty is the agent's sole motive for acting as he does, and that all his natural inclinations and leanings either are silent or militate against the dutiful act. Thus we can imagine a case in which someone refrains from violating a person's right despite the fact that he dislikes that person, that he would benefit from violating the person's right, and that he is not by temperament a warm or sympathetic individual. Kant thinks that we are prepared to consider the agent's conduct in such a case to be morally worthy, if we are convinced—rightly or wrongly—that he really is acting out of a sense of duty, rather than out of some hidden desire that the act promises to satisfy in some unobvious way. Indeed, Kant thinks, if we *are* convinced that the person is acting out of a sense of duty, then we are likely to be all the more impressed with the moral quality of his motivation, given that it is opposed to his own natural inclinations and interests and must therefore overcome them in order to be effective.

Supposing that Kant is right to say that motivation by a sense of duty is ordinarily distinguished from motivation by sentiment or inclination, mightn't the sense of duty nevertheless be thought of, compatibly with our ordinary understanding of it, as one of our natural attitudes or desires more broadly construed? Kant's conviction that this question must be answered in the negative derives from his understanding of the relations among morality, reason, and freedom, and complementarily among nature, determinism, and the absence of freedom. And this understanding too he takes to be continuous with our ordinary views.

As I have already implied, Kant does not think that we are always correct when we judge that a particular person has on a given occasion acted from a sense of duty. Indeed, he does not think we can be sure that we are ever correct. As is well known, Kant insists that it is easy to make mistakes about people's motives, so much so that we cannot be certain that we have ever actually encountered even a single instance of someone's acting from a sense of duty. Moreover, Kant understands as well as anyone that the very idea of motivation by a sense of duty, if understood as resisting assimilation within a naturalistic account, presents formidable difficulties. It is not easy to see how there could be such a thing as motivation independent of one's natural attitudes or inclinations. The fact remains, Kant thinks, that we do indeed ascribe to morality a kind of authority over our motives that is not dependent on what our natural attitudes or inclinations happen to be. If that is right, then any naturalistic account of moral motivation, including Hume's, really amounts to a denial of the existence of moral motivation as we understand it. That by itself does not imply that naturalism is wrong, only that it is inevitably skeptical or deflationary.[9]

Naturalistic accounts of moral motivation have become more sophisticated in various respects since the eighteenth century. Like other naturalisms, they have thrived as the intellectual prestige of the sciences has continued to grow. Some of these accounts are explicitly deflationary: that is, they accept a more or less Kantian interpretation of our prephilosophical conception of moral motivation, and claim to show that there is nothing in our actual motivations that answers to that prephilosophical conception. Others purport to be compatible with the correctness of our prephilosophical ideas as they understand them. For accounts of these two types, Kant's criticism of

---

9. It is natural to wonder about the extent to which Kant's conception of moral motivation is compatible with the claims I made in the previous chapter about the limited role of overtly moral considerations in human deliberation. It may seem obvious that, for Kant, motivation by a sense of duty always requires deliberation in explicitly moral terms. Recall, however, that my main claim in chapter 3 was simply that our use of verdictive moral language does not by itself commit us to saying that overtly moral thoughts should enter directly into agents' deliberations. As I emphasized, this is entirely compatible with the view that there are nevertheless circumstances in which, as a matter of fact, agents should indeed deliberate in overtly moral terms. Moreover, Kant's ideas about the extent to which motivation by a sense of duty requires such deliberation may be less clear-cut than they seem at first. One must distinguish between the way in which he takes the motive of duty to function in cases of morally required action, and the way in which he takes it to function in cases of morally permissible action. And even with respect to acts that are morally required, it is not obviously Kant's view that in all such cases people must explicitly test their maxims using the Categorical Imperative procedure; the idea that, without going through this procedure, one may sometimes know that one has compelling reasons to act in a certain way is not obviously uncongenial to him. (For suggestive if not conclusive discussion of these and related points, see the following papers by Barbara Herman: "On the Value of Acting from the Motive of Duty," *Philosophical Review* 90 [1981]: 359–82; "Integrity and Impartiality," *The Monist* 66 [1983]: 233–50; "Rules, Motives, and Helping Actions," *Philosophical Studies* 45 [1984]: 369–77; and "The Practice of Moral Judgment," *Journal of Philosophy* 82 [1985]: 414–36.) Nevertheless, Kant's complicated and sometimes obscure position may well be incompatible with some of the views I defended in chapter 3. My aim in the present chapter is not to defend Kant's overall position, but rather to explain why some of his views about moral motivation present a continuing challenge to naturalistic motivational accounts. In chapter 5 I will argue that sophisticated naturalistic accounts of a certain type may in fact have the resources to respond to Kant's challenge, and I see no reason at all to believe that *those* accounts must be incompatible with any of the claims I defended in chapter 3.

motivational naturalism presents two different challenges. For the purportedly nondeflationary accounts, the challenge is to explain how the truth of such an account is compatible with the correctness of our prephilosophical ideas, given Kant's argument about the antinaturalistic import of those ideas. The most straightforward way to meet this challenge would be to show that Kant is, to one degree or another, mistaken in his interpretation of our common understanding of moral motivation. Perhaps the idea that we are unwilling to count motivation by sentiment or inclination as moral motivation is simply a mistake. Or perhaps, although Kant is correct up to a point, he fails to see that there is some particular sentiment that differs in crucial respects from all others, and that we are prepared to recognize as a source of moral motivation. Or perhaps the sense of duty, although not analyzable as a sentiment or feeling, can nevertheless be reckoned, compatibly with our ordinary understanding of it, among our natural attitudes or desires more broadly construed.

For the explicitly deflationary accounts, the challenge is different. Obviously, such accounts are not embarrassed by Kant's claim about the incompatibility of motivational naturalism with our common understanding of morality, for they agree with it. The challenge, however, is to explain how the truth of such an account is reconcilable, not with the correctness of our prephilosophical ideas, but with our acceptance of those ideas. If, for example, moral motivation in fact consists in motivation by some natural attitude or inclination, how are we to explain the fact that people ordinarily conceive of the two as distinct? An explicitly deflationary account cannot meet this challenge by denying that people *do* ordinarily conceive of the two as distinct, for then it will cease to be deflationary. Instead, such an account must provide an "error theory": an explanation of why we think that motivation by a sense of duty is distinct from motivation by sentiment or natural attitude, even though it really is not.

Broadly speaking, then, Kant's criticism of motivational naturalism challenges both deflationary and purportedly nondeflationary naturalistic accounts to demonstrate their compatibility with our prephilosophical understanding of the motivational authority of morality. However, whereas the purportedly nondeflationary accounts must demonstrate their compatibility with the *truth* of our prephilosophical understanding, the explicitly deflationary accounts must demonstrate their compatibility with our prephilosophical *acceptance* of an opposed understanding. Despite the continuing popularity and increased sophistication of naturalistic accounts, such accounts still strike many people as dissatisfying. One reason for this, I believe, is that their responses to the Kantian challenge seem unconvincing to many.

Before explaining why, we must first raise the question of what the specific motivational sources of morality are, according to contemporary naturalistic accounts. Although such accounts vary in the responses they give to this question, two types of account are particularly prominent. Accounts of the first type are psychologically agnostic: they claim only that moral conduct is motivated by some "desire" or other (taking that term in the broad sense that is now standard in analytic philosophy), but they do not specify which desire or desires in particular do the job.[10] Accounts of the second type are more psychologically specific; they identify the relevant motivating factor as "sympathy," thus taking over a bit of eighteenth-century terminology that Hume used and with which Kant was familiar. I will refer to accounts of these two types as *standard naturalistic accounts* or simply *standard accounts*.

We may now observe that we have before us two independent distinctions within the class of standard accounts. First, there is the distinction between those accounts that are purportedly nondeflationary (or *nonrevisionist,* as I shall sometimes say,) and those that are explicitly deflationary. Second, there is the distinction between the psychologically agnostic accounts and what I will call the *sentimental* accounts, which see sympathy as the source of moral motivation. Since these two distinctions cut across each other, we have four types of standard account altogether: agnostic nonrevisionist (ANR), sentimental nonrevisionist (SNR), agnostic deflationary (AD), and sentimental deflationary (SD).

It is not difficult to understand why standard nonrevisionist accounts, whether agnostic or sentimental, do not seem to provide convincing responses to the Kantian challenge. Recall that the task for nonrevisionist accounts is to identify some natural attitude(s) that our prephilosophical understanding can be shown to regard as the source(s) of moral motivation, thus demonstrating how the truth of

10. This is something of an oversimplification, of course, since, strictly speaking, many such accounts identify motives with pairs of desires and beliefs, rather than with desires alone. For ease of exposition, I ignore this complication in the text, since it does not affect my arguments in any significant way.

such an account is compatible with the correctness of our pre-philosophical ideas. As I have indicated, however, ANR accounts remain schematic in that they hazard no opinion on the question of which specific kinds of desires motivate moral conduct. Instead they typically concentrate on trying to establish, on general philosophical grounds, the broader thesis that all conduct, and hence moral conduct in particular, is motivated by desire. In so doing, they clearly leave open the formal possibility of an adequate reply to the Kantian criticism, but they do not themselves provide one. Indeed, they tend not to address the criticism directly at all. SNR accounts, meanwhile, appear to be in a still less favorable position relative to the Kantian criticism. For they seem to be incompatible with one of the strongest elements in Kant's interpretation of our common moral understanding: namely, his ascription to us of a willingness to view an act as morally motivated even if the agent's temperament is not notably warm or sympathetic, and even if he must overcome considerable personal antipathy toward the beneficiary of his act in order to do what he does. It might of course be denied that we are willing to count cases like this as examples of moral motivation, but Kant's reading of our ordinary attitudes seems to me more persuasive on this point.

Standard deflationary accounts do not appear to fare much better in attempting to meet the version of the Kantian challenge that faces them. The task for deflationary accounts, as I have said, is to provide an "error theory" that will explain why we regard the sense of duty as different from any natural attitude or sentiment even though, on such an account, it really is not. AD accounts, however, again fail by virtue of their schematic character to take up this challenge directly at all. And SD accounts seem forced to maintain something of very dubious plausibility: namely, that our mistake consists in perceiving as a distinction between the sense of duty and any sentiment what-soever, including sympathy, something that is really a distinction between one form that sympathy can take, and all other sentiments, including other forms of sympathy. This would mean, for example, that the person who (as we might say) forces himself to do the right thing, even though he must overcome great personal antipathy to do so, should be seen as having had his antipathy outweighed by an even more powerful sympathetic tendency.

The difficulty that standard naturalistic accounts have had in meeting the Kantian challenge is less surprising than two other difficulties such accounts have faced. For the Kantian challenge, whatever its ultimate force may be, is in any event a challenge to motivational naturalism per se. By contrast, the other difficulties I have in mind are generated by the need to explain two phenomena that one might expect to be grist for the naturalist's mill, since they serve to illustrate the complex ways in which moral motives and beliefs are implicated in, and entwined with, important features of human psychology and social relations.

The first phenomenon is one I refer to as the *resonance* of morality. By this I mean the ramification of moral concerns throughout our mental and social lives. Consider, for example, the range of powerful human emotions and attitudes that seem both to be capable of spurring us to action and, in their central forms at least, to presuppose moral beliefs, in the sense that they could not be experienced by someone who had no such beliefs. Guilt, remorse, indignation, resentment, conscientiousness, and a sense of indebtedness all seem to fall into this category, for example. Thus, as a number of philosophers have pointed out, one can feel angry at being ill treated without having any moral beliefs, but one cannot resent the ill treatment unless one believes that it was wrong or unjustified or unfair.[11] And one can feel kindly disposed toward a benefactor without having any moral beliefs, but one cannot feel indebted unless one believes that one owes something to those who have treated one well. These simple observations, and others like them, testify to the fact that moral concerns, rather than constituting a self-contained element of human personality, are instead woven throughout the fabric of human emotion and motivation. They also testify to the interpersonal significance of moral concerns. For emotions and attitudes like those under discussion are important

11. John Rawls writes: "To deny that self-interested persons are capable of resentment and indignation is not of course to say that they cannot be angry and annoyed with one another. A person without a sense of justice may be enraged at someone who fails to act fairly. But anger and annoyance are distinct from indignation and resentment; they are not, as the latter are, moral emotions" (*A Theory of Justice* [Cambridge, Mass.: Harvard University Press, 1971], p. 488). And Bernard Williams says that, if an amoralist objects "to other people treating him as he treats them, this will be perfectly consistent so long as his objecting consists just in such things as his not liking it and fighting back. What he cannot consistently do is *resent* it or disapprove of it, for these are attitudes within the moral system" (*Morality: An Introduction to Ethics* [New York: Harper and Row, 1972], pp. 3–4). See also Joel Feinberg, "Justice and Personal Desert," in his *Doing and Deserving* (Princeton, N.J.: Princeton University Press, 1970), pp. 55–94.

elements in our repertoire of interpersonal responses; someone who actually lacked any moral beliefs, and who therefore never experienced such emotions, would be bound to strike us as humanly incomplete. Imagine, for example, a person who never felt guilt or remorse for his actions no matter what he had done, who never felt moral outrage or indignation at the ill treatment of another person by someone else, who never felt resentment no matter how badly or unfairly he himself had been treated or indebtedness no matter how well, and so on. Not only would such a person's repertoire of human responses strike us as significantly incomplete, but, moreover, this perceived incompleteness would tend to inhibit a range of significant attitudes and reactions toward him, including attitudes and reactions that did not themselves have independent moral presuppositions. It would thus raise doubts about the desirability, if not the possibility, of entering into various sorts of human interactions and personal relations with him. If this is right, it appears both that moral concerns are implicated in a wide range of human emotions and attitudes, and that a liability to experience these emotions and attitudes is in turn a prerequisite for participation in important human relationships of various kinds.[12] In this sense, moral concerns typically resonate, not only throughout the personality of the individual, but throughout the web of human social relations as well.

Standard naturalistic accounts, whether revisionist or nonrevisionist, offer no adequate explanation of these facts: no adequate account of how, given the content of our moral motivations, moral concerns come to have this kind of intrapersonal and interpersonal significance. Once again, the psychologically agnostic accounts, because they are schematic, contain nothing that obviously prevents them from providing an adequate explanation, but neither do they actually provide one. And the accounts based on sympathy are again in an even worse position. For, first, the resonance of morality casts

---

12. Rawls writes: "the moral feelings are a normal feature of human life. We could not do away with them without at the same time eliminating certain natural attitudes. . . . [A] person who lacks a sense of justice, and who would never act as justice requires except as self-interest and expediency prompt, not only is without ties of friendship, affection, and mutual trust, but is incapable of experiencing resentment and indignation. He lacks certain natural attitudes and moral feelings of a particularly elementary kind. Put another way, one who lacks a sense of justice lacks certain fundamental attitudes and capacities included under the notion of humanity" (*A Theory of Justice*, pp. 487–88). See also P. F. Strawson, "Freedom and Resentment," in his *Freedom and Resentment and Other Essays* (London: Methuen, 1974).

quite general doubt on the idea of moral motivation issuing from any one discrete sentiment or self-contained conative unit. And, second, it seems particularly incredible psychologically that *sympathy* should be the source of all our resentment, guilt, remorse, conscientiousness, and so on. In saying this, I am not forgetting that the sentimental tradition has devoted considerable effort to explaining how the sympathetic motive is capable of being engaged by the very wide and seemingly heterogeneous array of considerations that we regard as paradigmatically moral. Philosophers in that tradition have indeed worked hard to explain how such an apparently diverse collection of considerations—considerations of rights, fairness, justice, honesty, generosity, courage, benevolence, and so forth—could all seem salient to an individual by virtue of his being sympathetic. Hume, for example, argues at great length that, despite their apparent diversity, many such considerations have in common their utility, and that it is this utility that engages the sympathetic motive. However, the problem I am now discussing has to do with the adequacy of sympathy to explain the apparent variety and complexity, not of the considerations that strike us as paradigmatically moral, but rather of our own moral emotions and attitudes.

The second phenomenon that standard naturalistic accounts have difficulty in explaining is the psychological fragility of moral motivation: its ready liability to disfigurations and deformities of various kinds, and the psychological subtlety of the features that distinguish it from those disfigurations and deformities. The importance of this phenomenon for moral philosophy has often been emphasized by Richard Wollheim. Consider, as two examples of the phenomenon, the kind of behavior that we describe as "self-righteous," and the kind of attitude we classify as "excessively moralistic." In these two cases—each of which would repay closer examination than it has yet received from moral philosophers, or than it will receive from me here—our descriptions suggest that we regard morality as implicated, but in a distorted or inappropriate way, in a portion of the agent's motivational repertoire. Another example of the same thing is provided by the condition that Freud referred to, in a phrase borrowed from Nietzsche, as "pale criminality,"[13] a condition about which Wollheim has published an

---

13. See Sigmund Freud, "Some Character-Types Met with in Psycho-Analytic Work," in *The Standard Edition of the Complete Psychological Works of Sigmund Freud,*

illuminating and provocative discussion.[14] Pale criminality is the condition of one who commits a crime because of, rather than in spite of, its forbidden status, and for whom the crime, rather than producing guilt, helps instead to discharge it. Here too morality is implicated in a motivational pattern, but everything has gone wrong, it seems, with the way it is implicated.

Other examples of the disfiguration of moral motivation could be cited, but self-righteousness, excessive moralism, and pale criminality will suffice to illustrate my present point, which is that standard naturalistic accounts offer no satisfactory explanations of such phenomena. That is, they do not provide any adequate account of the evident psychological relationships between disfigurations like those I have mentioned and appropriate moral motivation. As usual, the psychologically agnostic accounts simply do not engage the question. And the sentimental accounts leave such disfigurations looking utterly baffling, incomprehensible. For one cannot plausibly represent phenomena like self-righteousness, excessive moralism, and pale criminality as transformations or distortions of the sympathetic motive. None of them can plausibly be diagnosed as a matter of too much sympathy, say, or too little, or selective sympathy, or misplaced sympathy. The point seems rather to be that none of them has anything much to do with sympathy. Yet each of them seems clearly to stand in some important psychological relation to appropriate moral motivation, and so the very existence of these phenomena casts doubt on the adequacy of sentimental accounts.

If some form of motivational naturalism is to be compelling, it will need to explain phenomena like resonance and fragility better than the standard accounts do, and to provide a more effective response to the Kantian challenge. And to the extent that objections to CO depend on one or another of the standard accounts, such objections cannot be fully persuasive. For the shortcomings of those accounts render them incapable of providing an adequate basis for the rejection of CO, and suggest that we do not yet have a fully satisfactory naturalistic interpretation of the authority of morality. Indeed, on the level of phenomenology at least, we do not yet have a

---

ed. James Strachey (London: The Hogarth Press and the Institute of Psycho-Analysis, 1953–74), 14: 311–33.

14. "Crime, Punishment, and Pale Criminality," *Oxford Journal of Legal Studies* 8 (1988): 1–16.

naturalistic interpretation of the authority of morality that is as convincing as the kind of broadly Kantian view in which CO is most naturally embedded. However, CO is, as I have indicated, such a strong claim that, despite its credentials on the level of moral phenomenology, there remains ample room for doubt about its acceptability, and ample motivation for exploring the prospects of a more successful naturalistic view. In the next chapter I will pursue these ideas further.

FIVE

Reason, Psychology, and the Authority of Morality

If anyone were inclined to put forward the paradoxical proposition that the normal man is not only far more immoral than he believes but also far more moral than he knows, psychoanalysis, on whose findings the first half of the assertion rests, would have no objection to raise against the second half.

SIGMUND FREUD, The Ego and the Id

I have said several times that CO is a very strong claim. Its strength is a function of two things: the exceptionless character of the connection between morality and rationality that it asserts, and the ambitious conception of rationality on which it relies. The second of these factors requires additional comment. Normative judgments about the rationality or irrationality of particular actions represent judgments about the responsiveness or unresponsiveness of those actions to the rational considerations that the speaker believes to have been available to the agent. Such judgments obviously depend for their truth on some conception of what counts as a rational consideration. That is, they depend on some conception of the kind(s) of consideration to which reason requires responsiveness. Two conceptions that have been particularly influential, both of which we encountered in the previous chapter, are the *instrumental* and the *prudential* conceptions. According to the former, reason requires that we do whatever will best satisfy the desires we now have. According to the latter, reason requires that we do whatever will best promote our own interests. We have already seen that CO is almost certainly incompatible with a purely instrumental conception of rationality, since it is very implausible to suppose that morally acceptable conduct represents the best way of satisfying the desires of every agent. And given the assumption that moral requirements can conflict with the agent's interests, CO is obviously incompatible with a purely prudential conception of rationality as well.

CO requires for its truth a more robust conception according to which practical reason is sensitive to considerations other than those of instrumental suitability and prudential advantage. Such a conception need not deny that instrumental or prudential considerations ever provide reasons for action, but it must in any case insist on the existence of an independent class of rational considerations. If we accept the idea that nothing can count as giving us a reason to act unless it is capable of motivating us, then the claim of any class of considerations to provide reasons for action is hostage to the motivational efficacy of those considerations. Few people would deny that instrumental considerations have this kind of motivational efficacy, for virtually everyone agrees that we are capable of being motivated by the consideration that a candidate action will satisfy our desires. Prudential considerations are more controversial, since many people doubt whether such considerations are capable of motivating us independently of any desires we may have to promote our own interests, and so they doubt whether such considerations constitute an independent class of reasons over and above instrumental reasons. However, the existence of the additional reasons asserted by any conception of rationality robust enough to support CO is more controversial still, for in this case the independent motivational efficacy of the putatively reason–giving considerations is even more widely doubted. This means that the task for advocates of CO is a large one; an ambitious conception of rationality must be defended against influential rivals that have more widespread intuitive support, and the links between rationality so conceived and morality must be convincingly exhibited.

Having said this, I may now seem to have contradicted myself. On the one hand, I argued in the previous chapter that the account of moral motivation in which CO is most naturally embedded has strong credentials on the level of moral phenomenology, and that accounts of moral motivation associated with the instrumental conception appear, at least at first sight, to be incompatible with our prephilosophical understanding of morality. On the other hand, I have now said that the instrumental conception is the conception of rationality with the greatest degree of intuitive support, and that CO depends for its truth on a more ambitious conception of rationality whose intuitive appeal is more restricted. What I have said is not inconsistent, but it does reveal an apparent conflict in our thinking about reason and morality. On the one hand, the traditional understanding of morality in which CO is embedded, and which is itself intuitively well entrenched, does seem incompatible with a purely instrumental conception of rationality. On the other hand, the purely instrumental conception of rationality seems to many people more plausible, as a conception of rationality, than the kind of conception that would appear necessary to vindicate our traditional understanding of moral authority. Thus there is an apparent conflict between what might be called the morality of common sense and the rationality of common sense. This is a type of conflict that arises in other contexts as well, and that I have elsewhere discussed in connection with questions about the rationality of agent-centered restrictions.[1] To resolve such a conflict, one must either show that it is only apparent, or give up or modify at least one of the conflicting views.

CO cannot itself be reconciled with a purely instrumental conception of rationality. And although I am sympathetic with attempts to defend a noninstrumental conception of rationality of the kind that CO requires, in the hope of resolving the conflict in favor of our traditional understanding of moral authority, the task seems to me a daunting one, for the reasons already given. I am not optimistic about the prospects of carrying out the task successfully, although I do not wish to argue that it is impossible, and would be happy if my pessimism proved to be unfounded. Assuming for the moment that it is not unfounded, the conclusion toward which we seem driven is that the traditional conception of morality's authority is mistaken, and that we need to arrive at some alternative understanding. However, although I do want to pursue the question what kind of authority morality would have if CO were false, it is worth asking, as part of that inquiry, how central CO is to the traditional conception. For even if CO itself were not in the end defensible, it might be that there were other elements in the traditional view that made less ambitious demands on a noninstrumental conception of practical rationality. If so, those elements might be easier to defend, and might be retained even if CO were false.

1. See "Agent-Centered Restrictions, Rationality, and the Virtues," *Mind* 94 (1985): 409–19 (reprinted in *Consequentialism and Its Critics,* ed. Samuel Scheffler [Oxford: Oxford University Press, 1988], pp. 243–60), and also the Introduction to *Consequentialism and Its Critics,* pp. 1–13.

In this chapter I will offer two reasons for thinking that less turns on the issue of overridingness than some have supposed. First, even if morality were overriding, it still would not have the kind of authority that some would like it to have. And, second, even if it is not overriding, it may nevertheless have considerably more authority than some have feared. If these suggestions are correct, then some of the hopes with which the traditional view has been invested may be doomed, even if CO is true. On the other hand, some elements of the traditional view may be defensible, even if CO is false.

Thus, there are two questions that we need to investigate. What kind of authority would morality have if it were overriding, and what kind of authority would it have if it were not? Let us begin with the first of these. On any normative conception of rationality, there is a conceptual gap between *the agent's (actual) reasons for doing what he does* and *what there is reason for the agent to do* (what reasons ought to move him). That is just what it is for such a conception to be normative. However, the size of the gap can vary from conception to conception, and it may be measured in terms of the extent to which the behavior that a given conception rules out nevertheless retains its appeal for people. The greater the appeal, let us say, the greater the *normative significance* of the conception that rules the behavior out. Now the normative significance of the kind of conception that would be necessary to vindicate CO is bound to be quite high. For such a conception must hold that it is sometimes irrational to do what will best satisfy our desires or advance our interests; and yet the continuing appeal of such putatively irrational behavior is likely to be considerable. The fact that such a conception would have a high degree of normative significance helps to explain why the truth of CO would not secure the kind of authority for morality that some would like it to have.

Part of CO's appeal for many people is that it seems to offer a philosophical guarantee of morality's hold on us. Depending on the kind of guarantee that is wanted, however, it is either the case that the desire for such a guarantee could not be satisfied even if morality were overriding, or that it could be satisfied even if morality were not overriding. Note that if reason requires that morality be given priority over concern for one's own good whenever the two sorts of consideration diverge, this implies that behaving in accordance with reason is not always good for a person. Now if rationality is characterized in such a way that it does indeed require people to give morality this kind of priority, then it can truly be said that people who persist in pursuing their own advantage in such situations are acting irrationally, at least insofar as they are aware of all the relevant considerations. But, as we have seen, their behavior may still be said to be guided by reasons, and reasons moreover of a perfectly recognizable kind. Often we will have no difficulty in seeing the appeal of the actions they choose to perform. Certainly their behavior in these situations need not strike us as peculiar or bizarre, and their behavior in other situations may well fail to manifest any other sort of irrationality. Thus to the extent that the desire for a guarantee of morality's hold on us is a desire to ensure that sane human beings will, insofar as their behavior is guided by reasons, always behave morally, or try to at any rate, it is doomed to frustration. One simply cannot guarantee by sheer force of philosophical will that sane people will always behave decently; or if one can, it is only by dint of some definitional fiat that deprives the claim of its intended force.

But, it may be said, if CO is true, then it is at least the case that all sane human beings can in principle be persuaded that they ought rationally to do what morality requires, that they act irrationally if they knowingly fail to do so. Consider, however, how much weight is borne in this formulation by the phrase 'in principle'. There is no suggestion that all sane people will in fact be persuaded. It may be true that, if morality is overriding, then those who act wrongly because they are not persuaded, together with those who are persuaded but act wrongly anyway, can be regarded as violating a philosophical code of rationality. However, it is not clear why those sympathetic to morality should take much comfort from the suggestion that its authority rests exclusively on the possibility of charging wrongdoers with this kind of cognitive misdemeanor. There may well be more comfort to be had from a psychologically realistic account of the role that moral concerns and their sources play in the range of actual human lives.

If this seems like a surprising suggestion, that is due in part to the persistent influence of a naively egoistic psychology of the individual, often presented as a kind of no-nonsense view, a psychology for the hardheaded, which sees human motivation as having a substantial core of pure self-interest. The self-interested core may, compatibly with this view, be said to consist either in powerful self-interested desires, or in a strong tendency to be motivated by self-interested considerations independently of one's desires. On either interpretation, the view has often seemed to allow only three possible ways of trying to establish a place for morality in the psychology of the individual. The first strategy is to emphasize the self-interested advantages of morality, thus making its motivational appeal parasitic on the influence of the core motivation. The second strategy is to identify the psychology of morals with the human capacity for practical rationality, in the hope that that capacity may be strong enough to counteract the motivational power of self-interest. And the third strategy is to locate some other-regarding sentiment or desire on the margins of human nature, and to use it as a kind of affective peg from which moral concerns may be draped, however loosely, over the self-interested core. Each of these strategies may have something to be said for it. However, the underlying psychological picture is sufficiently simplistic that it should not seem unreasonable to expect the array of possible strategies itself to be altered by a finer-grained understanding of human personality. And this in turn may have a significant bearing on questions about the nature of morality's authority.

I take the inadequacy of naive psychological egoism of the kind just discussed to be confirmed by the phenomenon of resonance discussed in the previous chapter. The mere existence of that phenomenon shows that the naive picture of human beings as fundamentally self-interested is at the very least oversimplified, and that if we try to arrive at a description of morality's place in the structure of human motivation by asking how it ever comes to exert any influence over people whose dominant motive is pure self-interest, we will surely go astray. For we will already have failed to notice a fact that must be central to any adequate description: namely, that when moral concerns are present, they are, as I put it in the last chapter, woven throughout the fabric of human emotion and motivation.

This point, and the corresponding point about the way in which moral concerns resonate throughout the web of human social relations, bear directly on the question of what kind of authority morality would have, if CO were false. For these points strongly suggest that the falsity of CO would not mean, as some have perhaps feared it would, that a person was free simply to repudiate the motivational authority of morality. One reason why the kind of challenge to the authority of morality embodied in the question "Why should I be moral?" seems serious rather than frivolous or idle, is that it grows out of an apparently genuine doubt on the part of some people about whether morality has any claim on them. They wonder whether there is anything about the way they are that gives morality a purchase, so to speak. And one thing that contributes to this doubt is the relative ease with which some people apparently find that they can withhold their assent from any proposition they take to embody a moral judgment or principle. But if the observations I have made about the resonance of morality are correct, it may be difficult to avoid moral beliefs altogether. It may be difficult to avoid acquiring them in the first place, and, having acquired them, it may be difficult to lose them, even if these facts are sometimes obscured by the thought that having such beliefs is exclusively or primarily a matter of explicitly assenting to certain propositions. Perhaps there are people who lack moral beliefs, but one does not come to lack them as the result of a simple decision or act of will, nor would the falsity of CO imply otherwise.

These considerations already tell us a good deal about the kind of motivational authority that morality would have, if CO were false. They also suggest that, if we wish further to illuminate this question, we would do well to seek some realistic understanding of the role of moral concerns in human psychology and social relations. The failure of standard naturalistic accounts of moral motivation adequately to explain the phenomena of resonance and fragility, which we discussed in the previous chapter, was symptomatic of their failure to provide such understanding. However, given that the standard accounts also seemed incompatible with our pre-philosophical understanding of the authority of morality, their psychological inadequacy may actually be encouraging. For it leaves open the possibility that, if a more psychologically satisfactory account could be found, it might also be compatible with at least some elements of our ordinary understanding of moral authority. Indeed, it leaves open the possibility that, to some extent at least, the feature of the standard accounts that renders them incompatible with our ordinary thought about morality is not their naturalism, but rather their psychological inadequacy itself. Thus we need to ask whether a more satisfactory naturalistic account is available, and if so, what it implies about the authority of morality.

By contrast to the standard accounts, psychoanalytic theory is an example of a naturalistic theory of human motivation that has the resources to offer serious explanations of the phenomena of resonance and fragility. Of course psychoanalytic theory remains extraordinarily controversial despite its profound influence on our culture, and people who reject it outright will also reject its explanations of these phenomena. However, even if we do not in the end accept its explanations, the advantages of those explanations should still be evident, and should help to indicate some of the characteristics that satisfactory nonpsychoanalytic explanations would have to have. Moreover, these advantages suggest that, whether or not we accept psychoanalytic theory, investigating it may teach us something about the possibility of reconciling some sophisticated form of naturalism with elements of our traditional understanding of the authority of morality.

Many of Freud's writings touch on one or another aspect of the psychology of morals.[2] The classical Freudian account of moral motivation,[3] in broad outline, goes something like this. The repository of an individual's moral standards is the superego, a psychic structure that is formed in the young child as part of the process by which the child attempts to resolve its "Oedipus complex." During the Oedipal period the child experiences intense sexual and aggressive wishes with respect to its parents. So intense are these desires, and so undeveloped is the child's grasp of the difference between wish and deed, that the child becomes greatly alarmed at the consequences that it imagines these desires will bring in their wake. It therefore seeks to withdraw some of the intense emotional energies that are focused on its parents, and it is aided in doing this by a process of identification with the parents. This process, which builds on already existing identifications, involves establishing within the self a psychic structure, the superego, that resembles certain aspects of the parents as the child perceives them. These aspects include, inter alia, parental prohibitions against the child's fantasied sexual and aggressive behavior, the very prohibitions responsible for the

2. The following works are especially significant (all references are to *The Standard Edition of the Complete Psychological Works of Sigmund Freud*, ed. James Strachey, 24 vols. [London: The Hogarth Press and The Institute of Psycho-Analysis, 1953–74]): "On Narcissism: An Introduction," 14: 73–102; "Mourning and Melancholia," 14: 243–58; *Group Psychology and the Analysis of the Ego*, 18: 69–143; *The Ego and the Id*, 19: 12–66; "The Economic Problem of Masochism," 19: 159–70; "The Dissolution of the Oedipus Complex," 19: 173–79; *Civilization and Its Discontents*, 21: 64–145; *New Introductory Lectures on Psychoanalysis*, 22: 5–182.

3. There is a reasonably clear statement of what I am calling the "classical Freudian account" in Charles Brenner, *An Elementary Textbook of Psychoanalysis* (New York: International Universities Press, 1955).

terror the child experienced in thinking about the consequences of its Oedipal wishes. The establishment of the superego has several important results. First, the prohibitions that previously issued from external authorities now issue from within the self as well: external commands have been internalized. Second, some of the aggressive and libidinal energies previously directed at the parents are replaced by intrapsychic emotions. For example, some of the love and admiration previously directed at the parents is now directed instead at that portion of the self that has been remade in their image: in Freudian jargon, a narcissistic cathexis replaces abandoned object cathexes. And just as important, some of the hostility and aggression previously directed at the parents is now directed by the superego against other parts of the self, against the ego in particular, and is experienced by the child as guilt. Third, whereas previously the child's primary incentives to restrain its sexual and aggressive wishes were its desire to please its parents and its fear of displeasing them, now it is motivated, in part at least, by its desire to please its own superego (to please itself), and its fear of displeasing the superego (its fear of self-punishment). With time, as the child matures socially, emotionally, and intellectually, the superego is modified by new influences, typically including more realistic conceptions of the parents. As this happens, so too the child's moral standards develop and become more mature. The superego never altogether outgrows its origins, however, and the primitive elements that participated in its formative manifestations are always liable to reassert themselves under sufficient psychological pressure. And achieving an optimal balance among the superego and other psychic structures is invariably a difficult and delicate matter: developmental circumstances can all too easily lead either to an excessively strong superego or to a weak and underdeveloped superego, either of which is capable of making for considerable psychological trouble.

This brief summary overlooks many significant complexities, changes, problems, and obscurities in Freud's own various accounts of the psychology of morals.[4] And it ignores altogether the nu-

---

4. For example, I have deliberately abstracted from Freud's controversial views about the supposed differences in superego development between boys and girls, since the points I want to make about the psychoanalytic account of moral motivation in no way depend on those views. For criticism of Freud on this topic, see for example Nancy Chodorow, *The Reproduction of Mothering* (Berkeley: University of

merous modifications, variations, and alternatives that other psychoanalytic theorists have proposed. Even this brief summary,
however, incomplete and oversimplified though it is, suffices to
indicate why psychoanalytic theory has the resources to offer more
serious explanations than the standard accounts do of phenomena
like the resonance of morality and the disfigurations to which moral
motivation is susceptible.

Let me mention some of the most obvious features that enable the
psychoanalytic account to provide such explanations. First, the
theory represents the human personality as having a structure of
considerable complexity, and it locates the psychological basis of
moral motivation in the interplay between central elements of that
structure. Second, it insists that the impulse to restrain oneself that
moral motivation requires does not exist from birth and does not
come easily, but must instead emerge gradually out of a conflict
between powerful amoral urges directed at others and an even more
powerful wish for self-preservation. Third, by emphasizing the
central roles of imagination and internalization in the processes by
which this conflict arises and the capacity for moral motivation
emerges from it, the theory reveals the dependence of the end result
both on the vagaries of the child's intellectual and appetitive idio-
syncracies, and on highly contingent features of the child's
environment—including, most dramatically, the personalities of its
parents, but including also the makeup of other family members, as
well as the family's material, physical, psychological, and social
circumstances. Fourth, by representing the capacity for moral motivation as the product of conflicts among some of the most intense
motivations the young child has, and by emphasizing the hazards
and complications of the process by which the moral sense is
established, it makes it clear both that appropriate moral motivation
requires a delicate balance among powerful psychic forces, and that
where, as often happens, that balance is, to one degree or another,
imperfectly achieved, the results can be explosive.

In view of these features of the psychoanalytic account, I hope it is

---

California Press, 1978); Carol Gilligan, *In a Different Voice* (Cambridge, Mass.:
Harvard University Press, 1982); and Eli Sagan, *Freud, Women, and Morality* (New
York: Basic Books, 1988). See also, however, Juliet Mitchell, *Psychoanalysis and
Feminism* (New York: Pantheon Books, 1974).

clear why I think that psychoanalytic theory has the resources to offer serious explanations of the way in which moral concerns resonate throughout human personality, and of the ready liability of moral motivation to disfigurations and deformities of various kinds. We need not accept the theory to recognize the advantages of its explanations, or to agree that they provide a good indication of the complexity of the psychological materials from which any better explanations would have to be constructed. We may therefore bracket the question of psychoanalytic theory's ultimate acceptability, and treat the psychoanalytic account of moral motivation as an example of a naturalistic account that is more adequate psychologically than the standard accounts, which are either psychologically agnostic or psychologically insipid.[5] We may then ask whether anything can be learned from this example about the possibility of reconciling some sophisticated form of naturalism with at least some elements of our traditional understanding of moral motivation.

One way to begin is by considering whether psychoanalysis itself is in a better position than the standard accounts to respond to Kant's challenge to naturalism. It would appear that it is. For, on the psychoanalytic account, the commands of the superego are not guidelines for the satisfaction of some sentiment we feel toward other people. On the contrary, they have precisely the function of overriding sentiments, beginning with some of the earliest and most primitive manifestations of the strongest feelings we are capable of directing toward others. Thus psychoanalytic theory has no difficulty in agreeing with Kant that we distinguish motivation by a sense of duty from motivation by sentiment, or in agreeing that we

---

5. It may be suggested, however, that psychoanalysis stands in different relations to the agnostic and sentimental accounts. It is incompatible with the sentimental accounts, for the psychoanalytic and sentimental answers to the question of what in particular motivates moral conduct are inconsistent. By contrast, it may be said, there is no fundamental inconsistency between the psychoanalytic and agnostic accounts. For the latter, which are schematic, may be supplemented by some more specific answer to the question of what in particular motivates moral conduct, and the psychoanalytic account, it may be argued, represents one possible supplement. For this argument to be correct, however, it would have to be appropriate to interpret the psychoanalytic view as holding that moral conduct is always motivated by desire, since agnostic accounts, although schematic, do insist that the relevant motivating factor must be some desire or other. I shall soon be offering an alternative interpretation of the psychoanalytic account.

ascribe to morality a very special kind of authority over our motives. Moreover, it has no difficulty in explaining, in its own terms, why this is so. Some contemporary motivational naturalists have found it congenial to express their opposition to Kant by saying that morality consists of hypothetical rather than categorical imperatives. Revealingly, Freud formulated his own view differently. "Kant's Categorical Imperative," he wrote in "The Economic Problem of Masochism," is "the direct heir of the Oedipus Complex."[6] In *The Ego and the Id* he elaborated on this point:

> The superego owes its special position in the ego, or in relation to the ego, to a factor which must be considered from two sides: on the one hand it was the first identification and one which took place while the ego was still feeble, and on the other hand it is the heir to the Oedipus Complex and has thus introduced the most momentous objects into the ego. . . . As the child was once under a compulsion to obey its parents, so the ego submits to the categorical imperative of its superego.[7]

Even if psychoanalysis is in a better position than the standard accounts to respond to Kant's challenge to naturalism, however, that is not to say that it is compatible with our ordinary understanding of morality's authority. Indeed, the psychoanalytic account of morals is often taken to be highly deflationary, and its success in responding to the Kantian challenge may be seen as a triumph of deflationary motivational naturalism, which undermines rather than vindicates our prephilosophical conception of moral authority.

6. *Standard Edition* 19: 167.

7. *Standard Edition* 19: 48. Freud's reference here to the superego as "the first identification" may appear to conflict with my earlier remark that, in the Freudian view, the process of identification that forms the superego "builds on already existing identifications." However, elsewhere in *The Ego and the Id* (chapter 3) Freud himself suggests that the process of identification that forms the superego often consists in an "intensification" of an identification that is already present and predates the Oedipus complex. The apparent inconsistency between these two passages from *The Ego and the Id* appears to be resolved by some remarks that Freud makes in the *New Introductory Lectures*. There he says that the formation of the child's superego results from "a strong intensification of the identifications with his parents which have probably long been present in his ego," but adds that this "intensification" represents the first time that identifications are produced or strengthened in compensation for object loss, and that it therefore has a special "emotional importance" (*Standard Edition* 22: 64). The passage from *The Ego and the Id* that speaks of the superego as "the first identification," when placed in the context of the full paragraph from which it has been excerpted, admits of a consistent interpretation along the same lines, and this was presumably the interpretation that Freud intended.

It is true that Freud's own comments about morality often have a sharply critical character. Of course this is partly due to his preoccupation with the role played by an excessively harsh superego in the etiology of his patients' disorders, and other psychoanalytic thinkers have offered more optimistic interpretations of the implications for morality of psychoanalytical ideas.[8] Nevertheless, the traditional conception of the authority of morality hardly seems to be vindicated by the view that our motivation to behave morally derives exclusively from our fear of the superego's rage and our desire for its love and approval.

This formulation may be somewhat misleading, however, insofar as it represents psychoanalysis as identifying the moral motive exclusively with fear and the desire for approval. This overlooks the fact that the object of those attitudes, the superego, which is perceived as exerting pressure on the individual (not) to act in certain ways, is also part of the self. Thus it might be more accurate to represent psychoanalysis as identifying the moral motive with the entire complex consisting of the superego's demands and the attitudes they evoke. However, even this revised formulation may need modification. For Freud's characteristic emphases are developmental and clinical. He has a great deal to say about the origins of moral motivation in the young child and about the way it functions in severely neurotic adults. He has less to say about the structure of mature, nonpathological moral motivation, and it is not clear that the explanation in terms of fear and the desire for approval is meant to apply without modification to the latter case. Such an explanation would need to be reconciled with certain contrary indications, such as Freud's remark about the ego submitting to the categorical imperative of its superego. After all, categorical imperatives do not tell us what we must do in order to avoid punishment or to win love, and someone who acts in such a way as to achieve those aims is guided by hypothetical rather than categorical imperatives. Even if we allow for the partially ironic and deliberately revisionary character of Freud's remarks, there had to be something about the type of

8. See for example Heinz Hartmann, *Psychoanalysis and Moral Values* (New York: International Universities Press, 1960), and from a Kleinian perspective, Roger Money-Kyrle, "Psychoanalysis and Ethics," in *New Directions in Psychoanalysis,* Melanie Klein, Paula Heimann, and Roger Money-Kyrle, eds. (New York: Basic Books, 1955), pp. 421–39.

motivation he was discussing that called the categorical imperative in particular to mind.

In saying this, I do not mean to be claiming that the psychoanalytic account of morals is not in fact deflationary. Although the matter seems to me less clear-cut than it is sometimes taken to be, the idea that the psychoanalytic account is deflationary may in the end be correct. I shall not attempt to resolve this question. Still less do I wish to address the question of the overall theoretical acceptability of psychoanalysis. What I want to argue instead is that whatever its own merits may be, the psychoanalytic account of moral motivation suggests a way in which it may be possible to reconcile a sophisticated naturalistic account of some kind with at least one important element of our traditional understanding of morality. More specifically, the psychoanalytic account reveals that a sophisticated form of naturalism may be capable of denying that the only way in which a consideration can motivate someone to act is conditionally on the presence of a suitable desire. Freud's remarks about the categorical imperative are of interest in this connection because, when taken in the context of his theory as a whole, they suggest that there may be room within a naturalistic account for a distinction between such *desire-based* motivation and motivation that works in another way. The other way in which a consideration could motivate, according to this distinction, would be if the architecture of one's personality included an authoritative structure or set of standards, by virtue of which one regarded the consideration as providing one with a reason to act. Let us call this sort of motivation *authoritative motivation;* let us call the motivating consideration in such cases the *authoritative consideration;* and let us, purely for the sake of convenience, refer to the authoritative aspect of the self as the superego. Now, to see how authoritative motivation might work, let us suppose, as an example, that for someone whose superego took a certain shape, the fact that a given act would fulfill a promise was perceived as a reason for performing it. The suggestion would then be that this very perception could motivate such a person to act, without the interposition of an independent desire, by virtue of the authoritative status of the superego within the self.

It would be natural to object, at this point, that if indeed the superego has this kind of power, it must either be the repository of suitable motivating desires or else be capable of evoking such desires elsewhere in the self. However, from the standpoint of the motivational theory, there may be reason for resisting this suggestion. For a distinction between two different kinds of motivational influence—between desire-based motivation on the one hand and authoritative motivation on the other—may have its roots deep within the theory. Moreover, as Freud's remarks about the categorical imperative seem to me to indicate, such a distinction has strong phenomenological support. On the level of phenomenology there is all the difference in the world between undertaking an action in the hope that it will satisfy a certain desire, and acting in response to what one perceives as an authoritative consideration, which presents the performance of the act as a practical necessity. In cases of the latter type, the necessity typically seems to obtain quite independently of one's wishes, and often seems to conflict more or less sharply with those wishes. Of course, if a person does act in response to a perceived necessity, then it is appropriate to ascribe a suitable desire to the person: say, a desire to keep her promise. But, as Thomas Nagel has famously argued, the appropriateness of such an ascription in a case like this just follows from the fact that the person is motivated to keep her promise; it does not imply that the desire is what is motivating her.[9]

It may be objected that psychoanalytic theory in particular has no room for a distinction between desire-based and authoritative motivation, in view of the motivational role that it assigns to fear of the superego and a desire for the superego's approval. Or, to put it another way, the role assigned to those attitudes may seem to suggest that, for psychoanalytic theory, authoritative motivation is just a special case of desire-based motivation: a special case in which the motivating desire is to avoid or obtain a particular reaction on the part of the authoritative aspect of the self. As I have already in part suggested, however, I believe that the theory as a whole can be read in a different way. It can be read as supporting a genuine distinction between desire-based and authoritative motivation, but as insisting in addition on another distinction: between true authoritative motivation on the one hand, and motivation by fear of the authoritative self (or desire for its approval) on the other. According to this alternative reading, the latter form of motivation may, subject to the qualification about the complexity of its structure mentioned earlier, be regarded as a species of desire-based motivation. It is particularly

9. *The Possibility of Altruism* (Oxford: Clarendon Press, 1970), pp. 29–30.

prominent at early stages of development and in certain kinds of adult neurosis, though it undoubtedly manifests itself in virtually everyone at least some of the time. For it is a mark of a superego whose integration into the self is imperfect, and perfect integration is too much to hope for. But it is quite possible for a person to come on the whole to accept his own superego and to identify with it: to regard it as importantly constitutive of who he is. And, on the alternative reading, authoritative considerations may motivate directly in such cases, without the interposition on each occasion of the kind of fear or wish to please that is present when there is a reversion to a more primitive view of the authority within oneself. In saying this, the alternative reading does not deny that conformity to superego standards may be a source of deep and ongoing satisfaction to the agent, or that violations of them may cause severe distress; what it denies is only that one's motivation for responding to an authoritative consideration must always be the prospect of securing such satisfaction and avoiding such distress. For a mature person with a well-integrated superego—for a personality that takes a certain shape—the consideration itself can motivate.

Another aspect of psychoanalytic theory may help further to illuminate the distinction between desire-based and authoritative motivation. In psychoanalytical writings the concept of the superego is standardly paired with the concept of an ego-ideal. The putative relationship between the superego and the ego–ideal, and the relation of each to other aspects of the self, have been sources of confusion and disagreement ever since Freud first introduced the concepts.[10] 'Ego-ideal' is the older of the two notions, and Freud introduced it by describing a man as having "set up an *ideal* in himself by which he measures his actual ego."[11] At the same time Freud went on to distinguish such an ideal from the "special psychical agency which performs the task of seeing that narcissistic satisfaction from the ego ideal is ensured and which, with this end in view,

---

10. For discussion of Freud's differing uses of the terms 'superego' and 'ego-ideal', see Joseph Sandler, Alex Holder, and Dale Meers, "The Ego Ideal and the Ideal Self," *The Psychoanalytic Study of the Child* 18 (1963): 139–58; Roy Schafer, "Ideals, the Ego Ideal, and the Ideal Self," in *Motives and Thought: Psychoanalytic Essays in Honor of David Rapaport* (*Psychological Issues* 5, Monograph 18/19), ed. Robert Holt (New York: International Universities Press, 1967), pp. 131–74; and James Strachey, Introduction to *The Ego and the Id*, pp. 3–11.

11. "On Narcissism: An Introduction," *Standard Edition* 14: 93.

constantly watches the actual ego and measures it by that ideal."[12] Without attempting to survey all of the issues that have subsequently arisen about the relations between the ego-ideal and the superego, one can say that they all have roots in this original distinction, and in the continuing conviction of psychoanalytic theorists that an adequate account of the psychology of morals must make reference both to something like an ideal and to something like an observing, critical agency.[13]

For our purposes, the role assigned to an ego-ideal is interesting because it suggests an additional insight about the way in which authoritative motivation may work at least some of the time. If, abstracting again from the details of psychoanalytic theory in particular, we assume that the authoritative structure or aspect of the self includes an authoritative ideal of some kind, then the way in which some considerations may acquire motivational force is through their connection to that ideal. An action may be performed or rejected because it is perceived as required or excluded by considerations whose salience for the individual is explained by his or her internalization of the ideal. I do not mean that, case by case, one is motivated by the desire to live up to the ideal. The idea is not that one reasons: "I want to be a certain kind of person, to achieve a certain ideal.

---

12. Ibid., p. 95.

13. For discussions of these issues, see Jacob Arlow, "Problems of the Superego Concept," *The Psychoanalytic Study of the Child* 37 (1982): 229–44; Heinz Hartmann and Rudolph Loewenstein, "Notes on the Superego," *The Psychoanalytic Study of the Child* 17 (1962): 42–81; Edith Jacobson, "The Self and the Object World: Vicissitudes of Their Infantile Cathexes and Their Influence on Ideational and Affective Development," *The Psychoanalytic Study of the Child* 9 (1954): 75–127; Jeanne Lampl-de Groot, "Ego Ideal and Superego," *The Psychoanalytic Study of the Child* 17 (1962): 94–106; Samuel Novey, "The Role of the Superego and Ego-Ideal in Character Formation," *International Journal of Psychoanalysis* 36 (1955): 254–59; Annie Reich, "Early Identifications as Archaic Elements in the Superego," *Journal of the American Psychoanalytic Association* 2 (1954): 218–38, and "Pathological Forms of Self-Esteem Regulation," *The Psychoanalytic Study of the Child* 15 (1960): 215–32; Joseph Sandler, "On the Concept of Superego," *The Psychoanalytic Study of the Child* 15 (1960): 128–62; Joseph Sandler, Alex Holder, and Dale Meers, "The Ego Ideal and the Ideal Self"; Roy Schafer, "The Loving and Beloved Superego in Freud's Structural Theory," *The Psychoanalytic Study of the Child* 15 (1960): 163–88, and "Ideals, the Ego Ideal, and the Ideal Self"; Rene Spitz, "On the Genesis of Superego Components," *The Psychoanalytic Study of the Child* 13 (1958): 375–404. The distinction between the ego-ideal and the superego is correlated with the distinction between values (or goodness) and obligation (or "the ought") by Heinz Hartmann, in *Psychoanalysis and Moral Values*, pp. 27–28, and by Richard Wollheim, in *The Thread of Life*, chapter 7.

Therefore I must treat considerations of this type as decisive. These considerations militate in favor of act X and against act Y. So I will perform act X." Rather, the internalization of the ideal supplies the psychological background against which considerations of certain types are perceived as in themselves providing reasons for action. In other words, part of what it *is* to internalize an authoritative ideal is to come to perceive considerations of some kinds as providing reasons for action, and considerations of other kinds as having no deliberative weight whatsoever. Accordingly, for one who has internalized such an ideal, certain sorts of action present themselves as mandatory, while others are viewed as simply out of the question, as not representing serious options.

If a distinction between desire-based and authoritative motivation is accepted, what does it imply about the possibility of reconciling some form of naturalism with traditional ideas about the authority of morality? Such a distinction gives as naturalistic view the resources to acknowledge that there may be a genuine difference between motivation by a sense of duty and motivation by desire or sentiment. Moreover, to the extent that the contrast between hypothetical and categorical imperatives is a contrast between those considerations whose status as reasons is conditional on the presence of suitable desires and those whose status is not,[14] the distinction between desire-based and authoritative motivation enables a naturalistic view to accept the contrast, and to make sense of the traditional claim that moral imperatives are categorical. For the distinction gives a naturalistic view a way of agreeing that our reasons to behave morally do not all derive from or depend on our desires; in some cases no desire is present, and it seems natural to say that the authoritative consideration by itself constitutes our reason. Of course the Kantian distinction between categorical and hypothetical imperatives is also supposed to distinguish between considerations that provide reasons for any rational agent and those that do not. If we agree that nothing can count as a reason for a person unless it is capable of motivating him or her, then the distinction between authoritative and desire-based motivation does not answer to this part of the categorical/

14. In "Are Moral Requirements Hypothetical Imperatives?" (*Proceedings of the Aristotelian Society*, supplementary volume 52 [1978]: 13–29), John McDowell emphasizes the importance of this aspect of the contrast between hypothetical and categorical imperatives, and also its independence of claims about the irrationality of acting wrongly.

hypothetical contrast. For authoritative considerations, as they have been characterized, are capable of motivating only those people who have superegos of a certain kind. Such considerations motivate, so to speak, conditionally on the possession of a certain form of personality. This very fact, incidentally, would enable a naturalistic view to answer the most obvious objection to the idea that beliefs can motivate in the absence of desires. The objection is that for any belief we can think of, we can imagine someone holding that belief, but, in the absence of a suitable desire, not having any inclination whatsoever to act on it. And the answer would be that we cannot in fact imagine this in cases where the person's superego is such that the belief in question is an authoritative consideration for him.

At this point it may be worth restating the role played by the psychoanalytic account of moral motivation in the argument I have been presenting. Since I have taken no position on the truth or falsity of that account, the use I have nevertheless made of it may seem puzzling. It may be wondered whether the argument I have offered is really compatible with such agnosticism. I have already indicated why I believe that it is, but the point may bear explicit restatement. The psychoanalytic account, as I understand it, is a naturalistic construal of moral motivation that admits a distinction between desire-based and authoritative motivation, and that can in consequence accommodate part of our traditional understanding of morality. Even if psychoanalytic theory is regarded as false, the mere fact that it possesses these resources demonstrates that it is possible for a naturalistic theory to possess them. And even if the psychoanalytic account of moral motivation is regarded as being, on the whole, deflationary, despite the fact that it allows for a distinction between desire-based and authoritative motivation, such a distinction can be drawn independently of the psychoanalytic account in particular, and is available to naturalistic theories of other kinds. Thus we need not accept the psychoanalytic account in order to see it as teaching us something about the possibility of reconciling some form of naturalism with elements of our traditional understanding of the authority of morality.

It will be helpful to have a term for referring to those naturalistic views that accept a distinction between desire-based and authoritative motivation. I will speak of such views as *fine-grained* naturalistic conceptions. In chapter 4 I gave a general characterization of naturalistic conceptions of moral motivation as holding that our motivations for behaving morally stem ultimately from our natural attitudes, sentiments, or inclinations, or from other features of our psychology. We can now see that this formulation is slightly misleading. A fine-grained naturalistic account does indeed hold that our motivations for behaving morally all depend on, and in that sense stem from, our possession of certain kinds of psychological features. Equally, however, there remains an important sense, on such a view, in which these motivations may be said *not* to stem from features of our psychology. For such views make it possible to say that, given the shape of one's personality, one may sometimes be moved to act simply by one's perception of the external circumstances in which one finds oneself.

Relatedly, fine-grained naturalistic views generate pressure to modify the instrumental conception of rationality. For we have seen that such views make it natural to say that our reasons for action do not all derive from or depend on our desires, and the instrumental conception as it stands recognizes only reasons that are desire-based. At the same time, however, since fine-grained views agree that our reasons for action are all conditional on our possession of certain kinds of psychological characteristic, the modifications in the instrumental conception that they might inspire would not need to be as drastic as the revisions called for by Kantian conceptions of rationality.

It may be objected that I am exaggerating the differences between fine-grained naturalistic views and certain more familiar forms of motivational naturalism. In particular, it may be suggested that the standard accounts that I have described as agnostic are actually compatible with a fine-grained view. For, as we have seen, agnostic accounts hold that moral motivation is desire-based, but they do not specify which desires in particular are involved, and they use the term 'desire' in a sense that is much broader than the everyday sense. For example Bernard Williams, in an influential paper,[15] uses it "formally"[16] to refer to all the elements of an agent's "subjective motivational set,"[17] and he emphasizes that those elements may

---

15. "Internal and External Reasons," in *Moral Luck* (New York: Cambridge University Press, 1981), pp. 101–13. For an illuminating discussion of Williams's paper, see Christine Korsgaard, "Skepticism about Practical Reason," *Journal of Philosophy* 83 (1986): 5–25.

16. "Internal and External Reasons," p. 105.

17. Ibid., p. 102.

include "such things as dispositions of evaluation, patterns of emotional reaction, personal loyalties, and various projects, as they may be abstractly called, embodying commitments of the agent."[18] Thus agnostic accounts can readily agree that our motivations are not all desires in any very narrow sense, while nevertheless insisting that every action is motivated by some element of the agent's subjective motivational set and is desire-based in that sense. In this spirit it might be argued that the superego itself can be construed as one of the elements of a person's subjective motivational set, and that what I have called "authoritative motivation" can therefore be considered desire-based in the only sense of 'desire' that agnostic accounts require. Thus, it might be said, the distinction I have drawn between desire-based and authoritative motivation can be represented as a distinction within the category of desire-based motivation more broadly construed, and there need be no inconsistency between fine-grained naturalistic accounts and standard agnostic accounts.

If the term 'desire' were construed broadly enough, whether by explicit stipulation or by philosophical convention, then an argument of this kind might perhaps be successful. But the only way in which such an argument could hope to achieve success would be by sacrificing the capacity of agnostic accounts to provide illumination. For, as Williams himself points out,[19] a broad construal of 'desire' can be very misleading, and this argument provides an excellent illustration of the dangers. If the superego were subsumed under the category of desire, then it might perhaps be possible to represent authoritative motivation as a kind of motivation by desire. However, such a terminological maneuver would serve to blur an important distinction rather than to reveal a significant commonality. The distinction I have drawn between authoritative and desire-based motivation marks a genuine distinction in the psychology of action: a distinction that reveals itself on the level of phenomenology, and which answers to a contrast that plays an important role in traditional thinking about the authority of morality. Agnostic accounts, if interpreted as subsuming the distinction, would also encourage us to overlook it, for two reasons. The first is simply that their explicit focus is on what all instances of human motivation are said to have in common, even if that turns out to be nothing more in the end than

18. Ibid., p. 105.
19. Ibid., p. 105.

some form of reliance on some member of the agent's subjective motivational set. The second reason has to do with the particular choice of the word 'desire' to refer to all the disparate elements of the motivational set. Since the word is ordinarily used far more narrowly to refer to one type of element in particular, the effect of making it do double duty as a catch-all label is, almost inevitably, to produce an unconscious reductionist slide in which all the elements are thought of on the model of desires in the narrower sense. Certainly this does naturalism no service, since it creates a needlessly impoverished picture of the human motivational resources that the view is capable of recognizing, and invites the somewhat surprising conclusion that only a Kantian position can accommodate genuine motivational heterogeneity: that Kantian metaphysics may provide the only antidote for an oversimplified psychology.[20]

The objection we have been discussing alleged that I was exaggerating the differences between fine-grained naturalistic views and standard agnostic accounts. A complementary objection would be that I have exaggerated the degree to which a fine-grained naturalistic view can accommodate traditional ideas about the authority of morality. It might be said, in this spirit, that I have not given any reason to think that the considerations that are authoritative for an individual will always be moral considerations, in any plausible sense of that term. For I have not said anything that would rule out the possibility of someone's treating considerations as authoritative that would ordinarily be regarded as amoral, or morally eccentric, or even immoral. Nor does psychoanalytic theory, insofar as it provides the model for authoritative motivation, give us any reason to

---

20. Michael Smith, responding to a somewhat similar objection to the role assigned to desires in "Humean" accounts of moral motivation, writes:

> An attack of this kind on the Humean's argument is clearly not an attack on the *spirit* of his argument, it is rather an attack on the *details* of his argument. The Humean may therefore concede the details to the objector. That is, if *desire* is not a suitably broad category of mental state to encompass all of those states with the appropriate direction of fit, then the Humean may simply define the term 'pro-attitude' to mean 'psychological state with which the world must fit', and then claim that motivating reasons are constituted, *inter alia,* by pro-attitudes. ("The Humean Theory of Motivation," *Mind* 96 [1987]: 55)

Pace Smith, my objection is to the spirit of a view that regards the diversity of human motivation as a mere "detail." It is precisely this spirit that is responsible for the failings of the standard accounts noted in chapter 4, and that serves to discourage serious investigation of the motivational resources of naturalism.

think that such possibilities can be ruled out. If anything, it explicitly affirms these possibilities. So, it might be said, I am faced with a dilemma. Either the criterion for something's being a moral consideration is its having authoritative status for an individual, in which case any consideration may turn out to be moral, or else moral considerations constitute a mere subset of the class of authoritative considerations, with no more claim to categorical status, so far as anything I have said goes, than any other members of the class.

Recall, however, that my aim has been to see whether some form of naturalism might be reconciled with at least some elements of our traditional understanding of morality. And this aim, in turn, arose out of an ultimate interest in determining what kind of authority morality would have if CO were false. In this connection I have made the following points. First, phenomena like the resonance of morality provide evidence of how deeply implicated morality is in human personalities and social life. Most people are prone to experience a variety of emotions and attitudes that presuppose moral beliefs; they could not stop doing so in a wholesale way if they wanted to, nor would they want to, if they understood the place of such emotions and attitudes in the kinds of life we regard as good and the kinds of social relation we regard as desirable.[21] Second, not only do these facts themselves tell us something about the kind of motivational authority that morality would have if CO were false, but they also suggest that serious attention to the place of moral concerns in human psychology and social relations would help further to illuminate this question. Third, this last speculation is confirmed, at least in part, by reflection on psychoanalytic ideas about morality. For such reflection strongly suggests that any naturalistic account of moral motivation that was capable of explaining phenomena like the resonance of morality would also be capable of accommodating at least some traditional ideas about the authority of morality. In particular, such reflection enables us to see how moral concerns could, on a sophisticated naturalistic account, enjoy a kind of motivational authority that did not derive from their capacity to appeal to our desires. And this, of course, is one of the important kinds of authority that has traditionally been ascribed to morality. Now it is quite true that the considerations that are authoritative for

---

21. P. F. Strawson makes a similar point, though in a different context, in "Freedom and Resentment," which is included in his *Freedom and Resentment and Other Essays* (London: Methuen, 1974).

an individual, in the sense I have defined, need not in every case be moral considerations. This does indeed mark a departure from traditional ideas about the authority of morality, and it shows that the achievement of authoritative status is not by itself what makes something a moral consideration. There are independent criteria for determining what types of consideration count as moral. On the other hand, it seems clear that moral considerations achieve authoritative status with disproportionate frequency, and that this is due in part to distinctive features of those considerations, and in part to features of the internal authority itself. To put it another way, moral considerations have features that make them especially liable to attain authoritative status, given certain characteristic patterns of personality development.

These last points deserve emphasis. The role of the superego in authoritative motivation, as I am understanding it, is to confer motivational authority on certain types of consideration, particular instances of which may then serve to motivate the agent without the interposition of independent desires. This leaves open the question of why the superego confers authority on the particular types of consideration that it does. The fact that moral considerations attain authoritative status as often as they do, and the fact that they are so deeply enmeshed in our social and emotional lives, show that they have certain features that regularly, although not invariably, elicit such conferrals. The special status that morality would have even if CO were false derives, not from the mere fact that people sometimes treat moral considerations as authoritative, but rather from morality's possession of features that elicit conferrals of authority across a very broad range of actual human personalities. In other words, the authority of morality derives from its possession of properties that make it reason-giving for so many people.[22]

___

22. The general idea of authoritative motivation is compatible with a wide range of proposals as to what the relevant properties are. Suppose, however, that one believed both that CO was true, and that the authority of morality derived from the fact that moral principles were principles of pure practical reason. Then one could hardly agree that morality is capable of motivating only those agents who possess a certain form of personality that is not shared by all rational agents. Accordingly, one could not accept the idea of authoritative motivation as I have described it. On the other hand, the suggestion that an authoritative aspect of the self may play a role in moral motivation is not obviously incompatible in itself with the rationalist position. Offhand, for example, there seems to be no reason why one could not take the view that the (generic) superego is part of the psychological apparatus whereby purely

The upshot is that if CO were false, then, although morality would have less authority than it has traditionally been assigned, it would nevertheless have more authority than some have feared. Moreover, even if CO were true, and the traditional view were fully vindicated, morality would still not have as much authority as some might wish. For both these reasons, less may turn on the truth or falsity of CO than has often been supposed. And insofar as we are concerned with the question of how secure a place morality has in our lives, very little may turn on it. For, as we have seen, even the truth of CO would not guarantee that people will always behave morally, yet, at the same time, moral concerns are so deeply implicated in human mental and social life that the falsity of CO could hardly serve to dislodge them. Thus, as I said toward the beginning of the chapter, if we are looking for a philosophical guarantee of morality's hold on us, then, depending on the type of guarantee we are seeking, either our quest is doomed even if CO is true, or it can succeed even if CO is false.

This does not mean that the truth or falsity of CO is a matter of indifference. For anyone who is interested in the nature of practical reason, the question will continue to be of the first importance. And to the extent that we accept what I have been calling the "traditional conception" of morality's authority, the truth or falsity of CO will continue to matter a great deal to us. Perhaps CO can be given a satisfactory defense. As I have said, the task seems to me daunting, but the question remains open. My aim in this chapter has not been to argue against CO, but rather to suggest that, if it cannot in the end be defended, the implications for morality may be less devastating than some have supposed.

There will of course be those who disagree. Disagreement on this point, however, is compatible with agreement about the pervasiveness and moderation of morality. I have already offered an argument for pervasiveness; it is to the defense of moderation that I now turn.

---

rational considerations succeed in motivating rational human agents. On this view, the superegos of rational human agents confer motivational authority on moral principles in recognition of their status as principles of pure practical reason. Or in other words morality, by virtue of its rational status, elicits conferrals of authority from the superegos of all such agents. I do not explore this type of position in the text, because I am interested in the question of what authority morality would have if CO were false; but neither do I argue against it.

SIX

Purity and Humanity

As I noted in chapter 2, some of the leading traditional moral theories have in recent years been criticized as excessively demanding. The degree of a moral theory's demandingness is a function of a number of closely related factors. Two of these are especially important. One is the extent to which the theory's constraints are confining: that is, the extent to which they narrow the range of morally acceptable courses of action open to an agent. The other is the cost to the agent of satisfying the theory's requirements, which in turn is a function of such things as the degree of incompatibility, whether logical, physical, psychological, or practical, between what the theory requires the agent to do, and what it is in the agent's own interest to do.

This suggests that a given theory's level of demandingness may be subject to two sorts of variation. First, a theory may be more or less demanding on different occasions. Sometimes it may leave an agent with many acceptable options, and at other times with very few. On some occasions it may cost an agent very little to satisfy the theory's requirements, while on other occasions it may cost a great deal. Second, a theory may be more or less demanding of different individuals. Since the compatibility of different people's needs and desires with the theory's requirements may vary, the cost to different agents of satisfying those requirements may not be uniform. And since people in different circumstances may find different proportions of the activities open to them ruled out by the theory's constraints, the same theory may be more confining for some than it is for others.

In view of the two sorts of variability just mentioned, it may seem that we should forgo global talk about the relative demandingness of different moral theories in favor of more restricted judgments about how demanding such theories are for particular people at particular times. This overstates the case. Certain theories will on balance make greater demands of typical agents over the course of a lifetime than will others, and we may express this truth by saying that some theories are more demanding than others. What we must not do, however, is to forget that such global judgments do not tell us everything there is to know about the demandingness of moral theories. It is important to keep in mind, for example, that from the fact that one moral theory is more demanding than another, it does not follow that the first theory will on every occasion demand more of an agent than the second theory. And it is also important to keep in mind that a single theory may demand much more of some people than it does of others. This point is easily obscured, if we focus on a different fact that has been much more widely attended to in contemporary philosophy: namely, that moral judgments and prin-ciples may have to satisfy some significant condition of formal universality. This provides a sense in which it seems natural to say that a moral theory must demand the same thing of everyone. There is a different and equally important sense, I have been suggesting, in which the theory may nevertheless demand more of some people than it does of others.

Perhaps it would not be too misleading to put the point this way: even if a theory demands the same thing of everyone, it may not be as demanding of some people as it is of others. What this means is simply that, even if a moral theory exhibits formal universality, neither the cost of satisfying its requirements, nor the extent to which those requirements are confining, needs to be the same for everyone. A principle which said that nobody should ever steal would (typically) cost the hungry more than the well-fed to observe. And a principle which said that nobody should ever eat meat would narrow the morally acceptable options open to a man shipwrecked on a desert island with nothing to sustain him but a year's supply of cured beef far more drastically than it would narrow yours or mine.

Bearing these caveats in mind, we may recall that someone who regards morality as *stringent,* in my sense of the term, will expect an adequate moral theory, if there is one, to be very demanding. Someone who denies that morality is stringent, on the other hand, will find less demanding theories more plausible. There is, of course, considerable variation among such theories. The least demanding theory of all, it seems, would be one which said simply that people may do whatever they please: that morality places no constraints whatsoever on people's conduct. However, some would deny that it is appropriate to call this a moral position at all, and it is in any case extreme. Alternatively, a theory might say that moral demands reduce to the demands of self-interested rationality: that one is morally required to do whatever will maximize the satisfaction of one's (independently specified) interests. Like the previous position, such a theory would be minimally demanding. For although, unlike the previous position, it sees morality as confining, as requiring quite specific courses of action, it also sees those requirements as duplicating what it takes to be the prior demands of self-interested rationality; it does not see morality as imposing any *independent* constraints. Like the previous position, moreover, it denies that morality ever imposes net costs on agents, that it ever requires them to do things that are not in their own interest.

The view that morality is *moderate,* which is the view I wish to defend, is different. Although there are many versions of this view, with significant differences among them, they all agree on two important points. The first is that, under favorable conditions, morality permits people to do as they please within certain broad limits, and that it therefore lacks stringency. The second point is that morality does nevertheless make demands and impose constraints: it prohibits some things, requires others, and imposes costs— sometimes very great costs—on agents. The view that morality is moderate is therefore intermediate between the minimalist position that morality imposes no independent constraints and no net costs on agents, and the maximalist position that it is stringent.

The conviction that morality is stringent is common among its critics, but also among many who consider themselves its friends. Thus the issue of whether morality is moderate or stringent cannot be identified with the question of whether it merits our allegiance or our antipathy. It is, instead, a question of how one conceives of the moral perspective, and people who share a common conception may nevertheless disagree strongly in their attitudes toward the perspective so conceived.

This point can be illustrated by considering the more specific view that morality is stringent but not overriding. On the one hand, this is a position advocated by some of morality's severest critics. They argue that the stringency of morality makes it harsh and unreasonable, and that reason therefore cannot require that we always satisfy its demands. In this view, morality's stringency is taken as evidence of its nonoverridingness: its limited authority as a price paid for its extreme demandingness. At the same time, however, the combination of stringency and nonoverridingness is also advocated by some who are very sympathetic to morality. They argue that the moral point of view is identified with a distinctive set of concerns, and that stringency is simply the result of representing those concerns faithfully. Precisely because of the distinctiveness of the moral perspective, they add, moral assessments are unlikely always to agree with judgments made from the standpoint of an individual agent's interests; and, human nature being what it is, there is no reason to suppose that it will always be irrational, in cases of conflict, for the agent to give his own interests priority, even though we might wish he would not. In this view, the stringency of morality derives from the distinctiveness of the moral point of view, while its lack of overridingness derives from the contrast between the distinctive concerns of the moral perspective and the realities of the individual's point of view. So here we have two positions that differ radically in their spirit, emotional tone, and orientation toward morality, but that attribute to it exactly the same properties.

As I have suggested, those who see morality as stringent tend to have a shared understanding of the nature of the moral perspective. Although they may have diametrically opposed attitudes toward it, they agree in attributing a kind of *purity* to the moral point of view. It is not easy to give a precise characterization of the relative notion of purity, but the intuitive idea is clear enough: morality's concerns are specific, distinctive, and in particular, sharply to be distinguished from the standpoint of the individual agent's interests. To those who attribute this kind of purity to the moral point of view, the idea that morality is moderate involves the confusion of supposing that morality's distinctive content is capable to being diluted by concerns external to it: concerns generated from, and appropriate to, the point of view of the individual agent.

Obviously, those who regard morality as moderate reject this ideal of moral purity. They do not regard the moral perspective and the point of view of the individual agent as identical. But they do take very seriously the fact that moral norms serve in the first instance to regulate the conduct of human beings. They believe, accordingly, that moral norms should be capable of being integrated in a coherent and attractive way into the life of the individual agent. And they regard this requirement as imposing a significant constraint on the content of morality. To them it is the idea of the "purity" of the moral perspective that is confused, at least insofar as it is understood to mean that morality has a content that is unaffected by its role in the lives of individuals.

In referring to these two divergent understandings of morality, we may speak, somewhat tendentiously, of the contrast between an Ideal of Purity and an Ideal of Humanity.[1] How is the issue that divides these two contrasting ideals to be resolved? Those who are drawn to the Ideal of Purity have often defended their position in one of two related ways. The first is by appealing to some allegedly weak or uncontroversial property of moral claims or of the moral perspective, and by arguing that morality's stringency follows from its possession of this property. The second is by appealing to our common understanding of the nature of morality, as reflected in our ordinary use of moral language and our ordinary understanding of moral concepts. These are not the only ways in which the Ideal of Purity can be defended, and in the next chapter I will consider some others. But these two strategies have been employed often enough and have been influential enough that they merit careful examination at the outset. Let us consider them in turn.

In discussing the first argumentative strategy, I will focus directly only on its employment by utilitarian writers, although defenders of other demanding moral theories have sometimes used it too, and although I shall attempt to extract some more general lessons. One

1. It is hard to find good terminology in philosophy, and when you find some that you are satisfied with, it is likely already to have been used for some other purpose. Despite the Kantian assocations, 'pure' as I am understanding it is not contrasted with 'empirical', and the term 'Ideal of Humanity' does not refer to the principle that we should treat people as ends. Also, some writers have felt that the term 'purity' aptly characterizes Kant's conception of moral motivation, moral value, and the moral attitude more generally. Thus Bernard Williams, in *Ethics and the Limits of Philosophy* (Cambridge, Mass: Harvard University Press, 1985), pp. 195–96, uses the term to describe a cluster of putatively Kantian ideas that he regards as characteristic of the modern moral outlook. Again, however, my use of the term is not meant to suggest interpretive claims of this kind. The question of whether Kant's own view is closer to the Ideal of Purity or the Ideal of Humanity is one that I do not plan to address. For an independent discussion of different conceptions of moral purity, see Frances Myrna Kamm, "Purity in Morals," *The Monist* 66 (1983): 283–97.

of the most common versions of the strategy, as employed by utilitarians, is to attempt to argue from a formal property of universality or universalizability to the stringent utilitarian conclusion. Starting, in other words, from the premise that moral claims must be universal or universalizable in some sense, some utilitarians have attempted to derive the stringent normative principle that constitutes the heart of their theory: namely, that the right act in any given situation is the one that produces the best overall outcome, where outcomes are ranked from best to worst by reference to a principle that gives equal weight to the interests of everyone. As part of this effort, utilitarian writers have sometimes claimed that agent-centered or agent-relative principles, which differ from utilitarianism by making rightness and wrongness at least partly independent of considerations of overall value, and which are the hallmark of moderate moral outlooks, straightforwardly violate an uncontroversial requirement of universality.[2] The idea is that since, for example, such principles may tell me that I have a special duty to certain particular people, or a prerogative to devote attention to certain of my own particular projects out of proportion to their weight in any impersonal calculus, they violate the basic formal requirement that moral principles must apply to everyone and must not be tailored to specific individuals. But this is of course a confusion. Agent-relative principles do not apply to me or any other individual in particular; they quantify over everyone and they therefore apply to everyone in the only sense in which it is at all plausible to suppose that they are formally required to do. Thus, for example, what I have elsewhere[3] called an "agent-centered preroga-

2. I have discussed agent-centered or agent-relative principles in the following writings: *The Rejection of Consequentialism* (Oxford: Clarendon Press, 1982); "Agent-Centered Restrictions, Rationality, and the Virtues," in *Consequentialism and Its Critics,* ed. Samuel Scheffler (Oxford: Oxford University Press, 1988), pp. 243–60; "Introduction" to *Consequentialism and Its Critics,* pp. 1–13; "Deontology and the Agent: A Reply to Jonathan Bennett," *Ethics* 100 (1989): 67–76; and "Prerogatives Without Restrictions," *Philosophical Perspectives* 6 (1992). In saying that such principles are the hallmark of moderate moral outlooks, I mean only that those theories that represent morality as moderate typically conceive of morality's moderation as achieved through the inclusion of agent-relative principles of certain types. Agent relativity is not a sufficient condition of moral moderation, for there can be exceedingly stringent agent-relative principles. Some people would argue that it is not a necessary condition either, and that some theories containing no agent-relative principles nevertheless represent morality as moderate. I myself do not find such arguments convincing, but I am not taking it for granted here that they are mistaken.

3. See the writings referred to in note 2.

tive" says that each agent is permitted to devote a certain proportionately greater weight to his or her own projects than would be licensed by an exclusive appeal to an impersonal calculus. This principle will of course have specific implications for the conduct of particular people in their individual circumstances, as will any moral principle, but what this establishes is its relevance rather than its nonuniversality.

Interestingly, the supposed incompatibility of agent-relative principles with a formal requirement of universality has been appealed to, not only by utilitarians seeking to discredit agent-relative principles, but also by people who take agent-relative principles for granted and seek to discredit some version of the requirement of universality. In other words, the supposed incompatibility is sometimes treated, not as an objection to agent-relative principles, but as a reductio of the universality requirement itself. It is in this employment that the claim of incompatibility has incurred the wrath of R. M. Hare, who writes:

> This objection results from a logical confusion: that between individual constants and bound individual variables. The principle that for all x, if x has made a promise, x ought to see that it is fulfilled, is as universal a principle as any; and so is the principle that for all x and y, if y is the mother of x, x ought to do certain sorts of things for y. No individual constant appears in them, and therefore moral judgments which rest on them are universalizable. It is surprising how seductive this confusion has been.[4]

There is some irony in the repudiation of this argument by Hare, since he himself attempts to argue from the requirement that moral judgments be universalizable to utilitarianism as a criterion of right action. However, he does so *via* an argument that, although not in my view successful, is independent of and more complex than the doomed appeal to the alleged formal nonuniversality of agent-relative principles.

Rather than appealing to a formal requirement of universality to bridge the gap between the concept of morality and the substance of utilitarianism, some utilitarians have appealed instead to the more intuitive notion of impartiality. They begin by arguing either that it is a conceptual truth, or else that it is at least an overwhelmingly plausible idea, that morality must be impartial. They then point out

4. R. M. Hare, *Moral Thinking* (Oxford: Clarendon Press, 1981), p. 140.

that what many agent-relative principles precisely do is to permit or require various forms of partiality to oneself, one's family, one's projects, and the like. By contrast, they claim, utilitarianism, which gives everyone's interests equal weight in the determination of what any given agent ought to do, embodies impartiality in its purest form.

Just as the alleged nonuniversality of agent-relative principles has been used by some to argue against such principles, and by others as a reductio of the universality requirement, so too the alleged partiality of agent-relative principles has been used by some to argue against those principles, and by others as a reductio of the idea that morality is impartial. Whichever direction they are pointed in, however, such arguments obscure more than they illuminate. This can be illustrated by considering the employment of one such argument in a recent defense of utilitarianism by David Brink.[5] Brink criticizes the suggestion that utilitarianism should be rejected in favor of principles that give more weight to the interests of the agent, or to the "personal point of view." Concerns about the personal point of view, he maintains, may lead us to challenge the authority of morality, but they should not lead us to doubt the utilitarian account of the content of morality, or to accept an agent-relative account in its stead. He gives two arguments for this position. Of these, the more substantial consists in the claim that utilitarian principles are superior to agent-relative principles, because they embody a kind of impartiality that matches our pre-philosophical understanding of the moral point of view.[6] Clearly,

---

5. "Utilitarianism and the Personal Point of View," *Journal of Philosophy* 83 (1986): 417–38. The portion of Brink's paper that I discuss here has been incorporated, with minor modifications, into his book *Moral Realism and the Foundations of Ethics* (Cambridge: Cambridge University Press, 1989), pp. 273–83.

6. Brink's other argument consists in the claim that incorporating the personal point of view into morality *via* an agent-centered prerogative, along the lines suggested in my book *The Rejection of Consequentialism,* makes it impossible to "represent . . . the conflicts between morality and the agent's interests with which we are familiar" ("Utilitarianism," p. 437), and thus renders the question of whether it is rational to do what morality requires unintelligible. This claim is clearly mistaken, since an agent-centered prerogative does not allow one to give unlimited weight to one's own interests, and since conflicts between morality and the agent's interest are, therefore, not only possible but inevitable on a view that incorporates such a prerogative. Brink says that an agent-centered prerogative as characterized in my book could conflict only with projects like "those of Caligula or Hitler" (p. 437n.). Since that version of the prerogative in fact makes the permissibility of pursuing any project at all dependent on the costs and benefits to oneself and others of

the success of this argument hinges on the account given of impartiality. According to Brink, utilitarianism assigns value impersonally, which means, among other things, that while it assigns value to people's commitments, it does not assign to a particular agent's "commitments any special value because they are *his*."[7] The agent's projects are important, but no more important than other people's. "In this way," Brink adds,

> the impersonal point of view is impartial. It is impartiality of this kind which we expect a moral theory to reflect. Nor is this kind of impartiality peculiar to utilitarianism or even to teleological moral theories. Many nonteleological theories recognize duties to forgo one's own good in order to prevent great harm to or provide great benefit for others. It is, of course, a substantive moral claim that it is this kind of impartiality which is characteristic of the moral point of view, but it is a plausible claim which cannot be rejected lightly.[8]

Notice that in these remarks Brink first associates impartiality with impersonality, which is said to involve the idea that the projects of all people are of equal importance and value. He then supports the claim that some nonutilitarian views exhibit "this kind of impartiality" by noting that they "recognize duties to forgo one's own good in order to prevent great harm to or provide great benefit for others." Thus the recognition of such duties appears to be treated here as *evidence* that a view exhibits impartiality, which is taken to be the property of assigning equal importance to the projects of all.

Despite the claim about the impartiality of some nonutilitarian views, Brink goes on in a subsequent passage to claim that "the impartiality among various people's goods which is characteristic of utilitarianism and other teleological theories represents important considered beliefs about the nature and demands of morality better than a . . . theory that incorporates the personal point of view into morality."[9] And of the "important considered beliefs" in question, he proceeds in the next sentence to identify one in particular: "An

---

the various options available to one, this is another mistake. It should be noted, moreover, that even if the prerogative did conflict only with "projects" like those of Caligula or Hitler, that would be sufficient to falsify Brink's claim that the prerogative makes questions about the rationality of moral demands *unintelligible*.

7. "Utilitarianism," p. 432.
8. Ibid., p. 432.
9. Ibid., pp. 435–36.

important moral belief is that the moral perspective is an impartial perspective; moral demands frequently require us to put aside purely personal projects and commitments in order to prevent harm or do good for others."[10] Notice now that, whereas the recognition of duties to forgo one's own good for the sake of others was previously presented as evidence that a view exhibits impartiality, which in turn was taken to be the property of treating everyone's projects as of equal importance, in this passage the impartiality we attribute to morality is directly glossed as the property of requiring "us to put aside purely personal projects and commitments in order to prevent harm or do good for others," and our belief that morality is impartial in *this* way is said to be best "represented" by "the impartiality among various people's goods which is characteristic of utilitarianism and other teleological theories."

The upshot is that impartiality is associated in Brink's discussion with two different ideas, the relation between which is characterized differently on different occasions and is to that extent obscure. The first idea is that everyone's projects are of equal value and importance. The second idea is that we must (frequently?) forgo our own projects in order to prevent (great?) harm or provide (great?) benefit for others. Whatever the relationship between these two distinct ideas may be, the relevant point for our discussion is that, insofar as the two ideas may plausibly be taken to reflect common moral opinion, those who accept agent-relative principles can happily endorse them both. With regard to the first idea, those who accept agent-relative principles do not claim that people are of unequal value or importance in impersonal terms, nor do they challenge the coherence or validity of such impersonal assessments of value. Although the claim that people are of equal value requires interpretation and perhaps qualification, there is nothing in standard agent-relative principles that even threatens to conflict with it. What those who accept certain agent-relative principles do deny is that an impersonal assessment of the value of a person's life or project must always exhaust its moral significance for that person; but they do not challenge the assessments of value themselves. In other words, they simply believe that one's own projects and interests can sometimes carry a disproportionate weight in determining what one may permissibly do, despite the fact that one is (obviously) no more

10. Ibid., p. 436.

important or valuable than other people. At the same time, as far as the second idea goes, those who accept agent-relative principles also believe that there are indeed circumstances in which one must forgo one's own projects in order to prevent harm or provide benefit to others. They do not regard moral assessments as simply coinciding with assessments of the agent's own interests. Utilitarians, of course, claim something even stronger than they do: namely, that one ought to forgo one's projects whenever one could thereby promote a greater net balance of overall utility (where overall utility is the aggregate of everyone's individual utilities, weighted equally). That stronger claim, however, just is utilitarianism; it can hardly be represented as embodying an uncontroversial conception of impartiality whose attribution to morality is one of our "important considered beliefs." Thus Brink's argument fails because, in the respects in which "we expect" morality to be impartial, agent-relative principles satisfy that expectation. And insofar as utilitarianism can be seen as embodying a more radical form of impartiality, it goes beyond any expectation shared by nonutilitarians. There is, in other words, no form of impartiality that (1) is uncontroversially viewed as a characteristic of the moral point of view, and (2) supports some form of consequentialism over agent-relative views.

This point may be made more vivid by looking at a wider range of the things that different people have in mind when they talk about the impartiality of morality. To begin with, some people who speak about impartiality mean to impute to morality some formal characteristic or other. Sometimes the characteristic in question is the property of universality, in which case the claim of impartiality reduces to the claim of universality previously discussed. But other formal properties may also be appealed to. As examples of *claims of formal impartiality,* therefore, we may take the following:

(1) Moral principles are universal in form; they quantify over everyone.

(2) Moral principles are general; they do not mention or refer to specific people.

Alternatively, the claim that morality is impartial is sometimes meant to convey the thought that people, or their goods or interests, are of equal value or importance from a moral point of view. This is clear from Brink's discussion. We may treat the following propositions as representative of what may be called *claims of value impartiality:*

(3) All human lives are of equal value or importance.

(4) The goods or interests of all people are of equal value or importance.

Remaining still within the broad category of value-impartiality claims, we also find assertions about the value impartiality of principles for the *aggregation* of value. Thus, for example:

(5) Overall states of affairs can be ranked from best to worst by reference to a principle that weights the interests of all people equally.

A third category of impartiality claims are those that assert some form of *normative* impartiality: that is, that represent morality as requiring us in certain contexts to act in ways that give other people's interests precedence over our own. Weaker and stronger examples, respectively, of such *claims of normative impartiality* are these:

(6) There are at least some circumstances in which the right thing to do is to give the interests of others priority over one's own interests.

(7) The right act in any given situation is the one that will produce the best overall state of affairs available to the agent, as judged by reference to a principle for ranking overall states of affairs that weights the interests of all people equally.

Finally, claims of impartiality are sometimes put forward as claims about the conditions that a person's *motives* must satisfy in order for what the person does to count as "moral" or "morally worthy." One example of a *claim of motivational impartiality* would be this:

(8) Moral conduct is conduct motivated by a sense of duty.

Clearly, in view of the variety of respects in which morality may be held to be impartial, there is enormous potential for confusion and equivocation in this area. Brink's discussion, for example, amounts to a vain attempt to construe the plausibility of the relatively more innocent propositions (4) and (6) as supportive of the highly controversial proposition (7), which is the utilitarian's distinctively strong claim of normative impartiality. And it is not only defenders of utilitarianism whose arguments sometimes suffer from a failure adequately to attend to the variety of forms that moral impartiality may be said to take. Attacks on the impartiality of traditional moral theories, including utilitarianism, have recently gained in popularity, but the allegedly problematic property is not always characterized in a clear and consistent way.[11] Similarly, the degree to which some nonconsequentialist theories share with consequentialism a common and controversial commitment to impartiality has recently emerged as an important and disputed question,[12] yet in my opinion, neither critics nor defenders of such theories have always distinguished among different forms of impartiality with sufficient care. Evidently, much remains to be said about the nature of impartiality. For the purposes of this discussion, however, the important point, as I have already asserted, is that there is no form of impartiality that is both uncontroversially associated with the moral point of view and also capable of supporting consequentialist over agent-relative theories.

In general, the strategy of defending the Ideal of Purity by attempting to derive the stringency of morality from some formal or uncontroversial moral property is doomed to failure. No truly uncontroversial property of morality implies that it is stringent. And no property that implies that it is stringent can be uncontroversially ascribed to it. I certainly have not proved these claims, and I have no

---

11. For criticisms of impartiality, see Lawrence Blum, *Friendship, Altruism and Morality* (London: Routledge and Kegan Paul, 1980), and "Iris Murdoch and the Domain of the Moral," *Philosophical Studies* 50 (1986): 343–67; Owen Flanagan and Jonathan Adler, "Impartiality and Particularity," *Social Research* 50 (1983): 576–96; John Kekes, "Morality and Impartiality," *American Philosophical Quarterly* 18 (1981): 295–303; Christina Hoff Sommers, "Filial Morality," *Journal of Philosophy* 83 (1986): 439–56; Bernard Williams, "Persons, Character and Morality," in *Moral Luck* (New York: Cambridge University Press, 1981), pp. 1–19. Also relevant are Alasdair MacIntyre, *After Virtue,* 2nd ed. (Notre Dame, Ind.: University of Notre Dame Press, 1984); Michael Sandel, *Liberalism and the Limits of Justice* (Cambridge: Cambridge University Press, 1982); Michael Stocker, "The Schizophrenia of Modern Ethical Theories," *Journal of Philosophy* 73 (1976): 453–66; Susan Wolf, "Moral Saints," *Journal of Philosophy* 79 (1982): 419–39.

12. In addition to the papers by Blum, Kekes, Sommers, and Williams cited in note 11, see Sarah Conly, "The Objectivity of Morals and the Subjectivity of Agents," *American Philosophical Quarterly* 22 (1985): 275–86; Nancy Davis, "Utilitarianism and Responsibility," *Ratio* 22 (1980): 15–35; Barbara Herman, "Integrity and Impartiality," *The Monist* 66 (1983): 233–50.

idea what a *proof* would look like. However, the strategy has never yet succeeded, and while it will probably continue to have its powerful allure for defenders of stringency, I am convinced that it is quixotic.[13]

I said earlier that adherents of the Ideal of Purity have often defended their position in one of two related ways, of which the attempt to derive stringency from some allegedly weak or uncontroversial or formal property of morality was the first. The second strategy involves an appeal to our ordinary use of moral language and our ordinary understanding of moral concepts. These two strategies obviously overlap to a certain extent, since the properties of morality from which stringency is said by the first strategy to be derivable are supposed to be weak or uncontroversial, and hence are presumably reflected in our ordinary speech and understanding. The second strategy becomes independent from the first, however, when it claims that what is embodied in our ordinary use of moral concepts is not the attribution to morality of some property from which stringency is derivable, but rather an explicit construal of morality as stringent.

In this employment the second strategy crucially depends on another appeal to the ambiguous notion of a *moral consideration*. The idea is this. In ordinary moral thought, it is claimed, personal considerations are one thing, moral considerations quite another. Personal considerations are considerations that have to do with one's own projects, plans, interests, happiness, and fulfillment, whereas moral considerations have to do with such things as fairness, equality, respect for rights, the keeping of promises, the discharging of obligations, a concern for the welfare of others, and so on. Moreover, it may be said, the one thing that unites the otherwise diverse class of moral considerations is the fact that they all derive from a set of norms that oppose and constrain the agent's pursuit of his or her own interests. Thus, this line of thought may continue, it is part of the concept of morality as we understand it that moral considerations stand in opposition to considerations of self-interest and per-

13. After explaining very clearly, in his book *Practical Ethics* (Cambridge: Cambridge University Press, 1979), what is wrong with the strategy, Peter Singer goes ahead and uses it anyway, though he does limit himself to the claim that it provides a "persuasive" rather than a "conclusive" reason for accepting utilitarianism. See pp. 10–13.

sonal advantage. Our very use of moral concepts embodies a construal of morality as stringent, because the function of those concepts is precisely to express demands that serve as a check on our otherwise unrestrained preoccupation with purely personal concerns.

Interpreted sympathetically, this line of thought reminds us that often what looms largest, in our thinking about morality, is the fact that it presents us with a distinctive set of demands and requirements that serve to restrict the pursuit of individual interests. Since those who view morality as moderate see it as including relatively robust permissions for individuals to attend to their own projects and plans, we can see how the prominence in our everyday thought of the restrictive and demanding aspects of morality might lead someone to conclude that the claim of moderation conflicts with our ordinary understanding of moral concepts. We can see how someone might conclude that those concepts represent morality as stringent. However, there are at least three reasons why it would be a mistake to draw these conclusions. First, the idea that morality is stringent is the idea that it is extremely demanding; and even if morality were ordinarily conceived of exclusively as a set of restrictions or demands, this would leave open the question of how difficult or burdensome it was to satisfy those demands. Second, as I have already argued, morality as ordinarily understood is best construed as permitting what it neither requires nor prohibits, and this implies that a construal of morality as consisting exclusively in a set of demands and restrictions is *not* built into our ordinary use of moral concepts. Third, the idea that morality includes not merely permissions, but relatively robust permissions, for individuals to attend to their own projects and plans, itself occupies a secure place in ordinary moral thought. For even if what are paradigmatically thought of as moral considerations do not include "personal" considerations, the fact remains that many people who devote more attention to their own projects and plans than a stringent morality would allow nevertheless regard themselves as morally justified in so doing. They do not see themselves as leading immoral or even morally neutral lives. Whether or not they are correct in these self-assessments, their conviction that they are morally justified in living as they do depends on the assumption that "personal" considerations can affect overall moral verdicts despite not counting as paradigmatically "moral," and shows that our ordinary use of moral concepts does not embody an unambiguous construal of morality as stringent.[14]

On the view that sees morality as moderate, the question of what an individual agent morally ought to do is certainly distinct from the question of what course of action would most enhance the agent's personal well-being, and the answers to these two questions sometimes diverge. At the same time, however, the types of considerations on which the two answers are based are not mutually exclusive, and the answers do not diverge in every instance. Instead, considerations about the agent's interests are among the considerations that help to determine what the agent morally ought to do, and overall moral verdicts often, although not always, coincide with assessments of personal well-being. On this view, the fact that "personal" considerations are not thought of as paradigmatically "moral" is explained precisely by the fact that such considerations are relevant to both sorts of assessment, and hence are not associated exclusively or distinctively with moral appraisal. It remains entirely appropriate, on this view, to think of morality as *constraining* the individual agent's pursuit of his or her own interests. All that is inappropriate is to infer from this that morality is always or usually hostile to conduct that promotes the agent's well-being. On the contrary, such conduct is, according to those who regard morality as moderate, often fully legitimate from a moral standpoint.

Those who regard morality as stringent do not in general deny that the interests of the agent count for *something,* morally speaking, since the agent is after all a person like any other. But they take a

---

14. Moreover, as we have already seen, and as is emphasized again below, even those who regard morality as stringent ordinarily agree that "personal" considerations can sometimes affect overall moral verdicts despite not counting as paradigmatically "moral." Thus the argument under consideration, if accepted, would appear to prove too much, for it would seem to show that "personal" considerations can never have this kind of relevance. In other words, if the argument supported the claim of stringency at all, it would support it only in an implausibly extreme form. Recall that in chapter 4 we examined an appeal to the notion of a moral consideration that purported to show that morality requires "humanly incorrect" behavior. That appeal, according to one interpretation, turned out to depend on just such an extreme form of the claim of stringency. The argument we have been examining here is different, because it appeals to the notion of a moral consideration in an attempt to *establish* that morality is stringent. In both cases, however, the ambiguity of 'moral consideration' serves to conceal the distance between the truism that "personal" considerations lack paradigmatic moral relevance and the implausible idea that such considerations can never affect overall moral verdicts.

dim view of the idea that one's own interests count for more than other people's in determining what one may permissibly do. They see this as amounting to a moral endorsement of our natural partiality, an endorsement that serves only to dilute the distinctiveness of the moral point of view. "Personal" concerns have enormous motivational power whatever their moral status, and it is not morality's business to make special accommodation for them.

I have argued that the second strategy for defending the Ideal of Purity is unsuccessful because it fails to establish that our ordinary use of moral concepts embodies an unambiguous construal of morality as stringent. Nevertheless, I do not wish to deny that the claim of stringency has roots in our prephilosophical understanding of morality. On the contrary, I believe that the claim of stringency and the claim of moderation both occupy recognizable places in our collective moral consciousness. Partly for that very reason, however, neither claim can be adequately defended by appealing either to formal properties of morality or to facts about ordinary usage.

In the next chapter I will defend the view that morality is moderate rather than stringent, in the only way that seems to me appropriate. I will try to set out the advantages of this way of thinking: the reasons for finding its construal of the institution and practices of morality attractive. Although both ideas have their place in our culture and traditions of thought, I believe that the understanding of morality in which the claim of moderation is embedded makes better sense of more of our moral thinking, and fits together more coherently with our deepest and most humane hopes and aspirations. What I shall offer, then, is not a proof but a proposal: a proposal that we think of morality this way rather than that, not because there is no precedent for the other way of conceiving it, or no argument for so doing, and not because I am convinced that morality is ours to shape as we please, but rather because this way of conceiving it coheres with more that matters to us—so that if there is a correct way of conceiving it, this is more likely to be it, and if there is not, then this is still the conception we have more reason to embrace.

SEVEN

The Case for Moderation

As we have seen, the idea that morality is moderate stands midway between two more extreme positions: between the view that morality is stringent and the view that moral requirements never genuinely conflict with considerations of overall self-interest, and so never impose any net costs on agents. Thus the claim of moderation represents an intermediate position. As against the view that morality and self-interest ultimately coincide, the intermediate position holds that there is the possibility of real conflict between them. As against the view that morality is stringent, the intermediate position holds that actual conflict is neither ubiquitous nor in general stark. Each of these contentions requires explanation and defense, and the defense of each must be shown not to undermine the defense of the other.

In chapter 4 I identified three different versions of the view that morality and self-interest ultimately coincide. The first of these defines morality in terms of the agent's interests, while the second defines the agent's interests in terms of the moral life. Thus each of these versions of the view sees the coincidence between morality and self-interest as conceptually guaranteed. By contrast, the third version sees the coincidence as a matter of empirical fact rather than of conceptual relations. Of these three versions, the third has perhaps the most in common with the view that I wish to defend, according to which the relation between morality and self-interest is one of potential congruence. For the latter view also holds that the extent of the convergence between morality and self-interest is in part an empirical question, and it agrees that the degree of conflict between morality and self-interest is often exaggerated, largely through reliance on excessively narrow construals both of individual interests and of the moral point of view. On the other hand, the suggestion that morality and self-interest always coincide, as a matter of empirical fact, seems implausibly strong, and there is no good reason to believe it. To be sure, political philosophers have often seen it as the proper function of government to bring about a convergence between self-interest and morality, or at any rate between self-interest and obedience to law. However, it is notoriously difficult to show that any government could ever achieve perfect convergence, and in any case, the fact that it is thought necessary for the state to bring about such convergence implies that, in the absence of a well-functioning government, conflicts between morality and self-interest actually do occur.

The second version of the view that morality and self-interest coincide, which defines the agent's interests in terms of the moral life, is very different. This version does not deny that morality can conflict with self-interest as it is conventionally or customarily understood, but instead offers an alternative interpretation of individual interests such that they are always, by definition, best served by acting in ways that are morally acceptable. Obviously, this position does not tell us how much sacrifice in conventional terms morality may require. Indeed, it makes it difficult to formulate the question, since whatever morality requires is said by definition not to be a sacrifice. To the extent that the question continues to strike us as important and substantive, we are bound to feel that this position attempts to define a genuine problem out of existence. And this suggests that we regard morality and the individual good as representing two logically independent evaluative standpoints whose relation to each other is a matter for serious substantive consideration.

If that is right, then the first version of the view that morality and self-interest coincide, the version that defines the former in terms of the latter, will strike us as equally unsatisfactory. One way of putting the difficulty with this version is to say that it gives the wrong explanation of other-regarding norms. It appears to say that what is wrong with killing an innocent person, for example, is that such behavior, or the disposition to engage in such behavior, does not contribute to the well-being of the agent. Even if we agree that a disposition of this kind does not in fact enhance the agent's well-being, however, that hardly seems like a full explanation of what is wrong with killing the innocent. Surely any adequate explanation must make reference to the effects of such behavior on its victims. It may be replied that this version should be interpreted as holding, not that killing the innocent is wrong because the disposition to do so has adverse effects on the agent, but rather that the disposition to do so has adverse effects on the agent because the behavior is wrong—by some independent standard. Once this is said, however, we have a different position. Morality is no longer being defined in terms of the agent's interests. Instead, the content of morality is being taken as independently fixed, and so the thesis that moral requirements never conflict with considerations of individual well-being must rest either on an empirical claim, as in the third version, or on a claim about the nature of individual interests, as in the second.

Whereas the second version of the view that morality and self-interest ultimately coincide ties the agent's interests so closely to moral considerations that it leaves us unable to make judgments about those interests that we in fact want to make, the first version ties moral requirements so closely to considerations of individual well-being that it leaves us unable to make judgments about the sources of those requirements that we also want to make. In the end, both positions fail for the same underlying reason: they do not give the two standpoints—the moral standpoint and the standpoint of prudence, or individual well-being—the degree of autonomy and mutual independence that they actually have in our thinking.

It may be suggested that there is a more plausible version of the view that morality and self-interest ultimately coincide. This version holds neither that the claim of coincidence is true by definition nor that it is simply an accurate empirical observation. Instead, it holds that one consequence of the best available theory of individual interests is that the good life must be lived within certain constraints, and that one consequence of the best available theory of morality's constraints is that observing them must contribute to the living of a good life. Thus, this position maintains, substantive theoretical investigation of the notions of morality and self-interest reveals the mutual interdependence of these notions, and in so doing provides the basis for the claim of coincidence.

Until the theories of morality and self-interest to which this position appeals are actually produced, it is clearly not possible to provide a definitive response to it. However, if we were not persuaded by any of the first three versions of the thesis that morality and self-interest ultimately coincide, we are likely to feel that there are objections to this position as well. For presumably the theories to which it appeals may legitimately be held accountable to the full range of our pretheoretical beliefs about morality and self-interest. And if we are impressed by the degree of autonomy and mutual independence that these two notions actually have in our thinking, then we have good reason to doubt that any thesis of interdependence strong enough to support the claim that morality and self-interest coincide is likely to emerge from theoretical investigation.[1]

If one accepts this conclusion, however, then the idea that morality is moderate, rather than seeming the natural alternative to the view that morality and prudence ultimately coincide, may in fact seem quite peculiar. For if we grant that morality and prudence constitute two logically independent evaluative perspectives, each with its own characteristic concerns, it may then seem odd to suggest, as those who regard morality as moderate do, that the moral perspective itself attaches weight to prudential considerations—considerations pertaining to the agent's interests. Once prudential considerations are regarded as defining an autonomous perspective of their own, it may seem implausible or even confused to maintain that they also exert an influence within morality. That is, it may seem implausible or even confused to suppose both that morality and prudence are two distinct and potentially conflicting perspectives, and that moral judgments are based in part on prudential considerations.

Despite these appearances, the idea that morality is moderate is neither confused nor, in my view, implausible. Take the question of confusion first. Morality and prudence represent two distinct perspectives, neither of which can be reduced to or defined in terms of the other. Each has its own characteristic concerns and priorities. In other words, each defines a sensitivity with a distinctive shape, in virtue of which certain characteristic types of feature are highlighted or perceived as salient in particular situations. But this does not mean that there cannot be any overlap between the types of consideration

---

1. On the relations between *eudaimonia* and other-regarding ethical considerations in Aristotle's thought, see Sarah Broadie, *Ethics with Aristotle* (New York: Oxford University Press, 1991), pp. 110–18; John McDowell, "The Role of Eudaimonia in Aristotle's Ethics," in *Essays on Aristotle's Ethics,* ed. Amélie Rorty (Berkeley: University of California Press, 1980), pp. 359–76.

that appear salient from the one perspective and the types of consideration that appear salient from the other. It is perfectly possible for each of the two standpoints to attach importance to considerations of some one particular type, though they may well differ about the reasons for attaching importance to such considerations, and about the degree of their importance in relation to other sorts of consideration. Nor is this merely an abstract possibility. For the moral standpoint represents a perspective on how a person should live his or her life, and it would be bizarre to suggest that that perspective attached no importance whatsoever to the person's own interests. In fact, as we have seen several times, not even those who regard morality as stringent ordinarily make such a claim. They do not deny that the agent's interests can ever have any bearing on an overall moral verdict about what the agent ought to do. To be sure, they believe that the agent's interests have less weight in determining such verdicts than those who regard morality as moderate maintain, but they nevertheless view the agent's interests as both morally and prudentially relevant, and any sane moral outlook must do the same. This leaves us with the important substantive question of how much weight the agent's interests actually have from a moral point of view: the question of whether morality is moderate or stringent. But this issue cannot be settled simply by observing that prudential evaluation already gives weight to those interests. That fact by itself is irrelevant.

Thus it is a mistake to suppose that, because considerations about the agent's well-being have prudential relevance and hence are not distinctively or exclusively relevant to moral assessment, they therefore lack moral relevance entirely. As I have already said on more than one occasion, this mistake is encouraged by our tendency to equivocate in our use of the term 'moral consideration'. When we use it to mean something like 'consideration of a type that is paradigmatically relevant to moral assessment', we quite naturally assume that considerations about the agent's well-being are not in general moral considerations. But then we sometimes conclude, invalidly and incorrectly, that such considerations are not moral considerations in the sense that they are altogether irrelevant to moral assessment.[2]

---

2. Since, as I have said, even those who regard morality as stringent typically grant that the agent's interests have at least some moral relevance, such a conclusion would in any case support the claim of stringency only in an implausibly extreme form, as I have emphasized in chapters 4 and 6.

However, I do not wish to suggest that opposition to the idea that morality is moderate derives exclusively from equivocation of this sort. Such equivocation is indeed implicated in the mistaken thought that the idea of moderation involves a straightforward confusion. Even after that is recognized as a mistake, however, the idea that morality is moderate may continue to seem implausible. For even if there is nothing confused about the idea that considerations pertaining to the agent's own interests are both morally and prudentially relevant, nevertheless some ways of distinguishing between the kind of relevance that they have from a moral point of view and the kind that they have from a prudential point of view may seem more natural than others. In particular, it may seem natural to suppose that, from a prudential standpoint, the agent's interests are ultimately the only ones that matter, while from a moral standpoint those interests do not, ultimately, count any more than anyone else's in determining what the agent ought to do. To put it another way, it may seem plausible to suppose that the prudential evaluation of action is wholly personal, whereas the moral evaluation of action is wholly impersonal. This would appear to support the view that morality is stringent, and to count against the idea that it is moderate.

The appeal of a purely impersonal construal of the moral standpoint does not lie solely in the formal attractiveness of the contrast between morality and prudence that results from such a construal. An impersonal construal is also directly responsive to one important strand in our substantive thinking about morality. In particular, it answers to a conviction that what morality most importantly represents is a form of radical self-transcendence. The moral point of view, according to this strand of thought, is a standpoint that one attains by renouncing any distinctive attachment to oneself, and by acting instead from a thoroughly selfless concern for all. Of course, on this way of thinking, morality may be very demanding, since it is true by definition that such extreme self-transcendence requires a willingness to sacrifice the ordinary interests and concerns of the self. But, it may be argued, it is no objection to this way of understanding morality to say that such self-transcendence may be difficult or impossible for most people—or, indeed, for any human being—to achieve or sustain. An ideal may inspire us even if it is unattainable, and striving to achieve it may uplift and improve us even if our efforts fail. If, by contrast, we take the unattainability of the ideal as a reason to modify it to fit our limitations, then all we will manage to do is to degrade the ideal, and to ensure that the motivational status quo is not improved upon.[3]

The idea that morality requires radical self-transcendence occupies a recognizable place in our traditions of moral thought, and because it does there is support in our thinking for a purely impersonal construal of the moral standpoint. Yet, despite this support, the considerations opposing such a construal seem to me in the end more persuasive. Those opposing considerations can best be brought out by giving a fuller description of the relevant alternative to the idea that morality represents the standpoint of pure impersonality. I take this alternative construal to support the specific claim that morality is moderate, as well as the broader claim that the relation between morality and self-interest is one of potential congruence. On the other hand, it is important to emphasize that in defending these two claims by reference to the alternative construal, I will not be arguing for any one particular moral theory or set of moral principles. Both claims are compatible with a wide range of theories and principles that differ among themselves in significant ways. The alternative construal, as I understand it, supports the view that any adequate theory must fall within this range, but it does not by itself suffice to select a single theory as preferred.[4]

---

3. This particular argument in defense of the idea that morality requires self-transcendence depends on an additional conviction that morality so understood is unobjectionable. The argument is, in effect, that it is unobjectionable to understand morality in this way because morality understood in this way is itself unobjectionable. As should be clear from the discussion in previous chapters, however, one might agree that morality requires self-transcendence, but argue that morality so understood is, in view of its demandingness, highly objectionable. If one took this position, one could obviously not avail oneself of the argument in the text to support one's conviction that morality does in fact require self-transcendence. However, my ultimate aim in this chapter is to argue in favor of the idea that morality is moderate, and it is important, for this purpose, to see the most favorable light in which the opposing view may be cast. That is why I highlight in the text the position of those who not only regard morality as requiring radical self-transcendence but also regard morality so understood as having considerable positive appeal.

The fact that morality is sometimes understood in such a way as to require radical self-transcendence is noted by Thomas Nagel in *The View from Nowhere* (New York: Oxford University Press, 1986), pp. 173 and 206.

4. Thus, in particular, I am not arguing here for a hybrid theory of the type described in *The Rejection of Consequentialism*.

What I have said about the compatibility of the alternative construal with a range of different theories applies to the impersonal construal as well. A purely impersonal construal is compatible with many different forms of consequentialism, and there are

According to the alternative construal, morality attaches unmediated significance to each of two basic propositions. The first proposition is that, from an impersonal standpoint, everyone's life is of equal intrinsic value and everyone's interests are of equal intrinsic importance. The second proposition is that each person's interests nevertheless have a significance for him or her that is out of proportion to their importance from an impersonal standpoint. On the alternative construal, moral norms reflect and attempt to balance these two fundamental propositions.

In the previous chapter I alluded briefly to some of the intuitive advantages that such a construal enjoys in comparison with a purely impersonal construal. Notwithstanding the place occupied by the idea of self-transcendence in our traditions of moral thought, it is a basic tenet of our commonsense moral outlook that we are justified in devoting some disproportionate degree of attention to our own basic interests, where these are construed as including our fundamental human needs as well as the major activities and commitments around which our lives are organized. In other words, we do not believe that the amount of attention that we may legitimately devote to our own families, friends, communities, careers, and commitments is fixed solely by reference to their advantages from a strictly impersonal point of view. Within certain limits, the very fact of their importance to us by itself provides a justification for attending to them disproportionately. Of course some people do in fact sacrifice their own interests to an extreme degree, but such sacrifices are regarded as supererogatory or morally heroic, and not as universally required. This does not mean that our commonsense moral understanding endorses unlimited attention to our own basic projects and activities, still less to our other wants and desires, for clearly it does not. The commonsense view is not that we may do whatever we please, but rather that we may, within limits, devote disproportionate attention to those things that matter most to us.

This conviction is so widely shared in our culture, and so deeply entrenched, that outside of philosophy it is scarcely even articulated, let alone explicitly challenged. And this despite the familiarity of the

---

nonconsequentialist moral outlooks with which it is compatible as well. For such a construal, as I have characterized it, says only that the agent's interests do not ultimately count any more than anyone else's in determining what the agent ought to do. And this does not rule out every type of agent-relative principle.

idea that morality requires radical self-transcendence, and the fact that many people are genuinely concerned about the moral quality of their lives. True, questions about the degree of personal sacrifice that morality requires are raised and discussed, although the culture as a whole attaches far less urgency to them at present than to various other moral concerns. Even when those questions are discussed, however, the discussion almost always takes for granted the legitimacy of devoting disproportionate attention to one's basic projects and commitments. It is typically concerned instead with the extent to which expensive discretionary purchases and pursuits are defensible at a time when so much of the human race is living in misery. Doubts are seldom raised about the permissibility of devoting some disproportionate share of one's emotional and material resources to one's job, one's family, one's friends, one's community, one's personal health and physical well-being, one's cultural or religious interests, or even one's preferred forms of leisure or recreational activity (unless they are unusually expensive or morally problematic for some special reason). Nor is the predominant view merely that such disproportionate attention is, within limits, permissible or justifiable. Beyond that, certain forms of disproportionate attention—to one's family or community, for example—are thought by many people to be what morality itself paradigmatically requires, and such requirements—or "special obligations," as they are sometimes called—are often taken as helping to define morality's opposition to the unrestrained pursuit of personal gratification and narrow advantage.

These commonsense convictions about the moral legitimacy of disproportionate attention to one's major projects, concerns, and commitments provide direct intuitive support for the alternative construal of morality, for that construal provides the most straightforward and convincing explanation of the legitimacy of such attention: namely, that morality itself aims to accommodate not only the equal value or worth of all people, but also the individual moral agent's naturally disproportionate concern with his or her own life and interests.[5] If, by contrast, a purely impersonal construal

---

5. These remarks apply without qualification only to our convictions about the *permissibility* of devoting disproportionate attention to our own projects. The alternative construal alone does not appear to provide a fully satisfying explanation of special obligations, for the fact that morality is sensitive to our naturally disproportionate concern with our own lives and interests does not by itself seem to explain why we are

of morality is accepted, then our commonsense convictions cannot literally be correct, although it might be argued that the actual behavior they purport to legitimate can instead be justified on the ground that such behavior serves indirectly to achieve the aims of a purely impersonal morality. Such arguments urge in effect that, appearances to the contrary notwithstanding, a purely impersonal construal actually supports the idea that morality is moderate. To my mind, such arguments are extremely implausible. And even if one does find them plausible, they do not alter the fact that our commonsense convictions themselves support the alternative construal.

Of course this hardly establishes that the alternative construal is correct. It is certainly possible to argue that our commonsense convictions about legitimate disproportionality are mistaken, especially since, as I have already agreed, the idea that morality requires self-transcendence also occupies a recognizable place in our thinking about morality. Our commonsense convictions about legitimate disproportionality constitute evidence rather than explanations of the alternative construal's appeal. We still need to know what plays the role with respect to the alternative construal that, if I am right, the idea of self-transcendence plays with respect to a purely impersonal construal. That is, we need to identify the underlying strands in our thinking about morality to which the alternative construal is responsive. If a purely impersonal construal answers to a conviction that morality represents a form of self-transcendence, the alternative construal answers to the idea that morality makes possible an important form of personal integration. For, as we have seen, the alternative construal depicts moral norms as sensitive both to the idea that people are of equal value and to the idea that each person's interests have a disproportionate significance for him or her. And

---

required to do certain things for those to whom we have special ties. However, if a satisfactory explanation can be found, it is likely to be entirely compatible with the alternative construal. For although, on that construal, there remains a question about why our ties to others should be thought to have the specific kind of moral relevance that special obligations embody, the general idea that such ties are of direct moral relevance is not in question. By contrast, as noted below in the text, a purely impersonal construal implies that our commonsense convictions about legitimate disproportionality cannot actually be correct. Thus to this limited extent, our conviction that we have special obligations also provides intuitive support for the alternative construal as against an impersonal construal.

this interpretation answers to a conviction that living morally is a realistic possibility for most people, and that what makes it a distinctive possibility is that it enables one to integrate a respect for the worth of others with one's naturally disproportionate concern to lead a fulfilling life oneself. On this way of thinking, it is a crucial feature of morality that it is motivationally accessible to normal moral agents: that living morally is a serious if not always easy option for normally constituted agents under reasonably favorable conditions. Of course, from a philosophical point of view, this requirement cries out for interpretation. However, we need not await such an interpretation in order to recognize the place of these ideas in our commonsense thinking about morality, or to see how strikingly they contrast with those elements of our thought to which an impersonal construal is responsive.

As I have said, the alternative construal supports the idea that morality is moderate. To avoid misunderstanding, however, it should be distinguished from a view according to which the claim of moderation represents, as it were, a concession by morality to motivational reality: a compromise whereby the requirements of morality are reduced or relaxed so as to make them more accessible to human beings with all their flaws and imperfections. Such a view is suggested by Nagel, when he speaks of the need to "strike a bargain between our higher and lower selves"[6]—a bargain whereby the "prior" claims of impersonal morality are modified "to accommodate the normal limitations of human nature."[7] On the alternative construal, by contrast, morality is addressed from the outset to human beings as they are. It affords them the prospect of integrating two different motivational tendencies, and it has no "prior" content that must be "reduced" or "modified" when it is brought into contact with human nature.

Its unapologetic opposition to excessive abstraction from the conditions of human agency constitutes one reason for saying that the alternative construal embodies an "Ideal of Humanity." However, there is also another reason, which corresponds to another aspect of that ideal. If the ideal consisted solely in the conviction that morality satisfies a condition of motivational accessibility, then it might be embodied just as fully by the position that morality can be

6. *The View from Nowhere*, p. 202.
7. Ibid., p. 204.

defined in terms of the individual agent's well-being. The difficulty with that position, as we saw, is that it gives the wrong explanation of other-regarding norms. From the vantage point of the alternative construal, in fact, its strengths and weaknesses are just the reverse of those associated with a purely impersonal construal. Whereas the latter accurately identifies the source of other-regarding norms but fails to insist on the motivational accessibility of morality, the former insists on the motivational accessibility of morality but fails to give an adequate explanation of other-regarding norms. This formulation reveals what, on the alternative construal, underlies the superficial intermediacy of the claim of moderation. Rather than representing a hapless compromise between two powerful but imcompatible extremes, that claim is seen as the outgrowth of a conviction that morality is sensitive both to the impersonal value of others and to our naturally disproportionate concern with our own lives, and that it therefore strikes a balance between the personal and impersonal points of view. Given this conviction, each of the two extreme positions, rather than seeming notably powerful or compelling, appears simply to be incomplete or one-eyed, for each of them omits one of the two basic factors to which morality is responsive. By contrast, the alternative construal, which is sensitive to both factors, embodies an Ideal of Humanity not only in the sense that it insists on the motivational accessibility of morality, but also in the sense that it expresses a particular normative conception of human life: a conception according to which human life is defined in part by a recognition of the value of others. A person who denies the value of others, or who sees them as having value only insofar as they contribute to the satisfaction of his or her own aims, is less than human in this frankly normative but nevertheless entirely familiar sense.

It should be clear from the preceding remarks that, although the alternative construal supports the claim that morality is moderate, there is nothing in it to justify moral complacency, or to suggest that the way in which we happen to distribute our energy and resources at present is morally privileged. On the contrary, because it interprets moral requirements as striking a balance between the personal and the impersonal standpoints, it lays a principled groundwork for the criticism of particular practices or ways of life as either excessively harsh or excessively indulgent. Obviously, the question of where exactly the balance is to be struck is not settled by the alternative construal alone. As I said earlier, that construal is compatible with a wide range of more detailed substantive theories about the content of morality. Those theories strike the balance in different ways, and since the alternative construal does not by itself constitute a sufficient basis for choosing among them, that choice must be made on other grounds. For present purposes, however, the important point is simply that the alternative construal provides no reason to suppose that the way we now live must be immune to moral criticism. Rather, it explains why certain types of criticism may in principle be pertinent and legitimate.

To this point, I have argued that the alternative construal and a purely impersonal construal both respond to important strands in our thinking about morality. It is noteworthy, however, that there is an apparent asymmetry with respect to the ability of each construal to accommodate the concerns to which the other is most conspicuously responsive. The alternative construal can to a considerable extent accommodate the idea of radical self-transcendence to which the impersonal construal responds, because the alternative construal allows for concepts of supererogation and moral perfection. In other words, the alternative construal is entirely compatible with a theory that recognizes radical self-transcendence as a worthy ideal to strive for, so long as the pursuit of that ideal is not regarded as obligatory, and so long as the theory includes a less demanding set of requirements that are taken to define a morally acceptable life. By contrast, it seems harder for a purely impersonal construal to accommodate the conception of personal integration to which the alternative construal is responsive. Admittedly some might argue, as we have already seen, that the impersonal construal, properly understood, actually supports the idea that morality is moderate rather than the idea that it is stringent. And if the impersonal construal is understood in this way, then it may indeed be able to accommodate concerns about personal integration. The difficulty, however, is not merely that this way of understanding the impersonal construal seems implausible; just as significantly, such an understanding enables the impersonal construal to accommodate concerns about personal integration only by depriving it of its original appeal. For if, as I doubt, the impersonal construal really does support the claim of moderation, then it does not embody the idea of radical self-transcendence after all.

It is debatable how deep this asymmetry goes, and I shall not place much weight on it. Proceeding instead on the assumption that each construal continues to have its own distinctive appeal, I want to suggest that the alternative construal nevertheless has roots in our moral thought that are broader and deeper than the impersonal construal. For even if the impersonal construal embodies an idea of radical self-transcendence to which we genuinely attach some importance, nevertheless that idea does not reflect the dominant reality of our moral practice. That is, it does not accurately reflect the role that morality actually plays in our lives.

I have already described some of the ways in which moral concerns enter into the constitution of our personalities and the structure of our relations with others. It is a mistake to conceive of our moral lives as consisting primarily in explicit moral reflection and in conduct directly inspired by such reflection. However important these things may be, especially for some individuals, they represent only one aspect of the role that morality plays in human life. As we have seen in earlier chapters, moral concerns influence our perceptions of salience and the content of our deliberations even when we are not thinking in explicitly moral terms. Moral beliefs are implicated in our emotional lives, insofar as the possibility of experiencing certain emotions depends on the presence of such beliefs, and insofar as the appropriateness of those emotions on particular occasions depends on the reasonableness under the circumstances of the beliefs in question. And morality helps to structure human social relations, not only in the obvious sense that individuals must observe certain moral constraints if social relations are to flourish, but also in the sense that the liability of others to have reactions that involve or presuppose moral beliefs is one of the conditions that makes it possible and desirable for us to enter into valued types of interpersonal relations with them.

But this does not exhaust the ways in which moral concerns enter into the fabric of human life. In chapter 5 I suggested that for a person in whom the capacity for moral motivation has been fully developed, moral concerns may come to enjoy a kind of motivational authority that does not derive from their capacity to appeal to the person's desires. In other words, morality possesses properties by virtue of which moral considerations become independently reason-giving for such people. This suggestion bears on the issue at hand in the following way. As a person acquires the capacity for moral motivation—as moral considerations become independently reason-giving for that individual—one thing that happens is that the person attempts increasingly to shape his or her projects, insofar as it is possible to do so, to avoid conflicts with moral requirements. But since one's projects and commitments help to determine what is in one's interests, this means that the individual in effect shapes his or her own interests in such a way as to avoid perceived conflicts with morality. The upshot is that, in addition to structuring our percep-tions and our deliberations, our emotions and our relations to others, moral beliefs also help to shape our projects, our commitments, and our interests themselves. In short, even when we are not thinking in explicitly moral terms, moral beliefs and concerns help to determine what we see and think, what we do and feel, and how we react and relate to each other; they help to determine the projects and activities around which our lives are organized, and what our good and our misfortune consist in. In all of these ways, they help to determine who and what we are.

These considerations provide support for the alternative construal as against a purely impersonal construal. For they suggest that the idea of morality serving an integrative function is not merely something that has abstract appeal for us; moral beliefs and concerns actually do help to shape integrated lives. By playing the various roles I have described, in other words, moral ideas do in fact enable people to integrate a respect for the worth of others with their naturally disproportionate concern to lead fulfilling lives them-selves. Obviously, this does not imply that moral ideas always perform this function successfully, or that integration is always satisfactorily achieved. The point is rather that this is a function that moral norms perform when they have been successfully inter-nalized. To put it another way, it is one of the aims of a reasonable moral education that they should come to perform this function.

By contrast, although the idea of morality as radical self-transcendence has its abstract appeal, and although it continues to be influential, the notion that morality represents a possibly unattain-able ideal that is distinguished precisely by its remoteness from normal patterns of agency and motivation does not reflect the dominant reality of how moral concerns actually function in human life. Moreover, to the extent that the idea of radical self-transcen-dence can be reconciled with that reality, the most natural way of doing this is by interpreting the aim of self-transcendence as a supererogatory ideal, in just the way that the alternative construal would allow.

Thus, if I am right, the alternative construal makes better sense of the totality of our moral thought and practice than does a purely impersonal construal. As I have said, the alternative construal supports the idea that morality is moderate, but it does not support a particular moral theory or tell us precisely how demanding moral norms are. What it does do is explain why it may in principle be legitimate to object to a given theory either that it is too demanding or that it is insufficiently demanding. It explains why both types of criticism have standing. As I have also said on several occasions, and as these remarks serve to remind us, the idea of moderation constitutes an intermediate position, which stands midway between the view that morality is stringent, on the one hand, and the view that morality and self-interest coincide, on the other. Unlike the latter, it holds that conflicts between morality and self-interest can and do occur. But, at the same time, it sees such conflicts as arising far less frequently than is implied by the former. What I have been suggesting in this chapter is that this intermediate position is supported by a conception of morality as sensitive both to our naturally disproportionate concern with our own lives and to the equal importance of all people. If one regards morality as responsive to both these considerations, one will naturally see it as conflicting with self-interest more often than those who regard it as responsive only to the first consideration, and less often than those who regard it as responsive only to the second.

It may be objected, however, that the argument I have given for the alternative construal casts doubt on whether that construal really does support the idea that morality is moderate. For, it may be said, if morally motivated individuals shape their own interests so as to avoid perceived conflicts with morality, then the potential for conflict between morality and the interests of the agent is eliminated. Thus if attention to the integrative role of morality provides support for the alternative construal, it does so in such a way as to suggest, not that morality is moderate, but rather that morality and self-interest coincide.

This objection is overstated, but it calls attention to an important point. If the alternative construal is accepted, then, in view of the argument I have given for that construal, there are two powerful factors, rather than just one, that reduce the degree of conflict between morality and the interests of the individual agent. Not only does morality itself aim in part to accommodate the interests of the agent, but at the same time agents who acquire moral motives try, in effect, to shape their own interests in such a way as to avoid conflict with morality. There is no doubt that this process of mutual accommodation serves significantly to attenuate the degree of opposition between morality and self-interest. Nevertheless, there is no reason to expect the complete elimination of conflict, if the alternative construal is accepted. Indeed, there is reason not to expect it. For, according to that construal, morality is not sensitive exclusively to the interests of the individual agent. And although suitably motivated individuals do indeed attempt to shape their projects and commitments, and thereby their interests, so as to avoid conflict with moral requirements, there is no reason to suppose that everyone will be so motivated. Moreover, the attempts of those who are so motivated may nevertheless fail, or succeed only imperfectly, for at least four reasons. First, an individual's understanding of what morality requires may be faulty. Second, a pursuit that has a relatively high potential for conflict with moral requirements may be particularly attractive for an individual, despite the fact that moral considerations are independently reason-giving for that individual. Third, unfavorable social circumstances may create situations in which there is only a very narrow range of projects that people can acceptably develop and pursue, thus making it unusually difficult for a person to shape his or her interests in such a way as to avoid conflict with morality. And, finally, unexpected changes in natural or social circumstances may have the effect of rendering morally unacceptable a continued commitment to projects and pursuits that were perfectly acceptable when acquired, thus creating a conflict between moral requirements and individual interests where previously there was none. Indeed, almost any project can come into conflict with moral requirements in some circumstances. The fact that a project would not originally have been undertaken, had it then conflicted with those requirements, is no guarantee that such a conflict will not subsequently arise.

In view of these considerations, the assertion that the alternative construal supports the claim of moderation may be reaffirmed. There is no reason to think that conflicts between morality and the interests of the agent can ever be entirely eliminated. Yet as we saw at the beginning of chapter 6, and as the foregoing reflections confirm, the extent to which a moral principle conflicts with an individual agent's interests may depend, not only on the content of the principle, but also on the character of the agent's interests and on the circumstances in which the principle is applied. And this implies that the extent to which conflicts between morality and self-interest arise is not fixed once and for all. In fact, both the frequency and the severity of such conflicts are to a significant degree subject to human control. For human practices and institutions help to determine the prevalence, both of the motivational patterns that lead people to try to shape their projects in such a way as to satisfy moral requirements, and of the factors that have the potential to frustrate such attempts. In other words, both the extent to which people are motivated to accommodate their interests to the requirements of morality, and the extent to which their attempts at accommodation meet with success, are affected by the prevailing social institutions and arrangements under which they live. For these reasons, the degree of conflict between morality and self-interest is in part a social and a political issue.

EIGHT

Morality, Politics, and the Self

I have suggested that conflicts between moral requirements and the agent's interests are both possible in theory and ineliminable in practice, but that they arise less often than they would if morality were stringent, and that their frequency and severity are to a significant extent subject to human control. When such conflicts do arise, it is natural to wonder what the agent has most reason to do. As we have seen, the claim of overridingness asserts that it can never be rational for a person knowingly to do what morality forbids, even if, in acting wrongly, the person is doing what would best serve his or her own interests. This is a very strong claim, and I have expressed doubts about its ultimate defensibility. Even if the claim is false, however, it does not follow, and I do not believe, that it is always irrational to behave morally when such conflicts arise, or that promoting one's own interests is always what one has most reason to do. Nor does it follow that most people will in practice make the self-interested choice. To put it another way, the fact that morality was not overriding would not mean that prudence *was* overriding, and it certainly would not imply that people were thoroughly self-interested. Thus, in expressing doubts about the claim that it is never rational knowingly to do what morality forbids, I have not been suggesting either that it can never be rational to act morally at the expense of one's own interests, or that people never in fact do so.

Despite my doubts, the claim of overridingness (CO) may of course be correct. If it is not, however, then, according to the view that I sketched in chapter 5, a person may nevertheless be motivated to act in accordance with moral considerations even at some net cost to himself. And there is no reason whatsoever to suppose that an adequate theory of practical rationality will regard such conduct as less than optimal from the standpoint of reason. On the other hand, neither are there any grounds for expecting that everyone will in fact be motivated to make such sacrifices, or for thinking that those who fail to do so must always be acting contrary to reason. Thus, assuming that CO is false, the relation between what an agent is morally required to do and what that agent has most reason to do will be variable rather than uniform, on the view I have defended. For that view interprets judgments about the rationality of moral conduct as sensitive to features of human psychology that are themselves variable. In order for CO to be true, by contrast, it would have to be the case that such judgments were unresponsive to psychological features of this kind, and that they were instead sensitive exclusively to characteristics shared by all rational agents. Thus those who accept CO disagree with those who reject it about the features of human agents to which judgments concerning the rationality of moral conduct are sensitive, and about whether the relevant features are universally shared among rational agents or can vary.

This disagreement has often been represented instead as a dispute about whether the rationality of moral conduct does or does not depend on the agent's existing desires. Those who reject CO are said to hold that it does, while those who accept CO are said to deny this. As my argument in chapter 5 implies, however, this way of representing things cannot be accurate, since those who reject CO may nevertheless agree that an agent can have reasons for acting morally that do not derive from his or her desires. Alternatively, it might be suggested that the disagreement I have identified is really a disagreement about whether moral reasons are internal or external. I am unhappy with this way of describing the matter, however. The distinction between internal and external reasons, as introduced by Williams, is shorthand for a distinction between two different ways of interpreting statements that ascribe reasons for action.[1] On the internal interpretation, such ascriptions imply, roughly, that the agent has a motive for acting; on the external interpretation, they do

---

1. See "Internal and External Reasons," in *Moral Luck* (New York: Cambridge University Press, 1981), p. 101.

not. What is internal or external, on this way of speaking, is the relation between a reason and a motive—or, more accurately, between a reason-ascription and a motive-ascription. Now, if one interprets defenders of CO as claiming that moral reasons can legitimately be ascribed to people who lack any motive at all for acting on them, then it is natural to conclude that what those who accept CO maintain, and what those who reject it deny, is that certain external-reason statements are true. As it happens, I believe that this conclusion is mistaken, because I do not accept the inter- pretation on which it rests.[2] Mistaken or not, however, such a conclusion is likely to be very misleading, if offered as a way of characterizing the disagreement I have described. For that disagree- ment concerns the types of mental states or attributes that must be present in order for reasons to act morally to be ascribable to the agent. If the disagreement is characterized using the language of internal and external reasons, it is almost certain to be misconstrued as a disagreement between those who think that reasons for acting morally depend on *some* mental state or property of the agent— something "internal" *to the agent*—and those who do not. It is clear that this formulation misrepresents the issue, since those who accept CO certainly do not deny that the ascription to an individual of reasons to act morally depends on some state or property of that

2. In rejecting this interpretation I have been influenced by Christine Korsgaard. In "Skepticism About Practical Reason" (*Journal of Philosophy* 83 [1986]: 5–25) she argues that Kantians can accept what she calls the "internalism requirement," according to which "[p]ractical reasons, if they are really to present us with reasons for action, must be capable of motivating rational persons" (p. 11). From the internalism requirement, she argues, it follows that "if we can be motivated by considerations stemming from pure practical reason, then that capacity belongs to the subjective motivational set of every rational being" (p. 21). This would mean that every rational agent did have a motive, in the sense that Williams requires in order for something to count as an internal reason, for acting on purely rational considerations. If Kors- gaard's argument is correct, defenders of CO need not be interpreted as claiming that moral reasons can legitimately be ascribed to people who lack any motive for acting on them; they may instead be understood to hold that every rational agent has a motive for acting morally. I have taken the internalism requirement for granted in chapters 4 and 5.

Note that the internalism requirement must be distinguished from *ethical internal- ism,* where this is understood as the view that judgments about what an agent morally ought to do imply that the agent has a reason (or in some versions, a motive) for so acting. Although, on the interpretation just advanced, defenders of CO accept both forms of internalism, neither form entails the other. To complicate matters, several other theses have also been advanced under the heading of ethical internalism, and the relations among the various doctrines so labeled are not always clear.

individual. On the contrary, they insist that there is something about rational human agents by virtue of which they—as opposed, say, to cats or personal computers—have reasons to behave morally. To be sure, the relevant properties are thought by those who accept CO to be ones that all rational human beings share, but that is precisely my point. The most straightforward way to describe the disagreement between those who accept CO and those who reject it is simply to say that the disagreement concerns the features of human agents to which judgments about the rationality of moral conduct are sensitive, and the question whether the relevant features are or are not universally shared.

Having previously seen that the conception of morality for which I am arguing represents an intermediate position with respect to the frequency of conflict between morality and the interests of the agent, we can now see that it also represents an intermediate position with respect to the rationality of moral conduct in those conflict situations that do arise. On the one hand, it holds that there need be nothing irrational about giving moral requirements priority over one's own interests; but on the other hand, it sees no basis for the claim that this is always what people have most reason to do.

The intermediacy of the position in these respects should not be thought to imply a kind of bland optimism about the prospects for morality in our social world. Indeed, the conception of morality that I have been defending is much less likely than some other conceptions to encourage such an attitude. As we know all too well, the world can be an unbearably sad place, and people's astonishing capacity for deliberate cruelty and brutality is one of the most striking things about them. These facts are hardly news outside of philosophy, but on the whole it cannot be said that contemporary moral philosophy has displayed much interest in them.[3] Its focus on questions about the relative motivational importance of reason as compared with sympathetic or benevolent feeling has made it easy for philosophers to neglect the importance of sheer human viciousness: to forget that the desire to harm other people is one of the most prominent and enduring forces in human social life. Similarly, moral philosophy's emphasis on questions about the relative importance of happiness and pleasure, as compared with values of other kinds,

---

3. Stuart Hampshire's work, most notably *Innocence and Experience* (Cambridge, Mass.: Harvard University Press, 1989), constitutes an important exception.

makes it possible to forget the extent to which loss, grief, and feelings of despair are fixed features of the human condition. Its neglect of these facts is part of a more general tendency within moral philosophy to overestimate the efficacy of moral thought, a tendency which, as I argued in chapter 5, is also implicated in the idea that the overridingness of morality would somehow guarantee its hold on us. When moral philosophy does not overestimate the efficacy of moral thought, however, it tends often to underestimate it, as when it reduces moral values to mere desires and construes moral motivation as a matter of arbitrary preference, or when it denies that morality represents a distinctive evaluative standpoint that is not reducible to prudence or an enlightened self-interest.

The view of morality that I have been defending encourages a more balanced and realistic appraisal of the social role of moral thought. It acknowledges the existence of genuine conflicts between moral requirements and agents' interests, and provides no guarantee that reason will always insist on resolving such conflicts in morality's favor, still less that people will in fact always choose to resolve them in that way. At the same time it emphasizes the potential motivational power of moral considerations, and insists that the psychological bases of effective moral motivation have sources deep within the self. And it holds that neither the prevalence of the relevant psychological structures nor the degree of conflict between morality and the agent's interests is fixed and immutable. Both are strongly influenced by social institutions and practices that are not themselves unchangeable. And since the strength of one's reasons for acting morally may in turn depend both on the structure of one's psychology and on the degree of conflict between one's interests and morality's demands, the rationality of moral conduct is also affected to a significant degree by the character of the social and political institutions under which one lives. We might even overstate the case somewhat and say that, on this view, the overridingness of morality is neither conceptually guaranteed nor absolutely ruled out; it must instead be a social achievement.

There may appear to be an inconsistency between these ideas and my remarks in earlier chapters about the resonance of morality. For the upshot of those earlier remarks was that various forms of human social relationship presuppose moral beliefs, whereas the present suggestion is that the prevalence of effective moral motivation is something that depends on the character of social institutions. Thus it may look as if I have said both that moral beliefs make social relationships possible, and that the institutionalization of various social relationships makes moral beliefs possible. However, there is no inconsistency in what I have said. In the first place, the fact that various types of fundamental human relationship would be difficult or impossible to achieve in the absence of moral beliefs does not mean that the acquisition of the relevant beliefs occurs independently of all social institutions. There is no inconsistency in the idea that social institutions have a role to play in fostering those beliefs that are in turn required if certain basic sorts of human relationship are to flourish. And in any case, the factors whose variability and dependence on social institutions I have asserted above are not the same as the moral beliefs and concerns whose resonance I emphasized earlier. I have spoken of variation in the degree of conflict between morality's demands and the interests of the agent, and in the extent to which people are motivated to act morally, especially when doing so requires a net sacrifice from them in self-interested terms. Both forms of variation are compatible with the idea that people normally experience a range of emotions and attitudes that presuppose moral beliefs, and that the failure to do so would tend to inhibit certain important types of interpersonal relationship. In particular, the fact that most people reveal through their emotions that they have moral beliefs is compatible with the existence of substantial variation in the extent to which people are actually motivated to behave morally. For although a failure ever to be motivated by moral considerations would certainly cast doubt on one's possession of moral beliefs, the possession of such beliefs does not by itself guarantee that moral motives will always be one's strongest motives, or that one will always be motivated to act as morality requires. For one thing, the possession of such beliefs does not by itself mean that one attaches highest priority to moral values, or that one cannot in good faith assign greater weight to considerations of other kinds in situations of conflict. In addition, there is room for hypocrisy, self-deception, and other forms of bad faith, all of which testify to our capacity for selective and self-serving application of the principles that we accept. There is also the phenomenon of simple moral weakness. All these considerations support the conclusion that people who possess moral beliefs may vary considerably in the extent to which they are motivated to satisfy moral demands. Nor is there any inconsistency between these considerations and my suggestion in chapter 5 that moral beliefs can by themselves motivate a person to act, for my suggestion was only that this could happen under certain psychological conditions, not that it must happen whenever such a belief is present. Similarly, my claim that moral beliefs help to shape the interests of people in whom the capacity for moral motivation has been fully developed does not imply that the mere presence of such beliefs guarantees the existence of effective moral motivation.

As I have said, the suggestion that the overridingness of morality must be a social achievement overstates the implications of my position. Nevertheless, it is an illuminating overstatement, and one that is worth examining in greater detail. We have seen that social institutions have the capacity to influence the rationality of moral conduct both by nurturing the psychological bases of effective moral motivation, and by reducing the degree and frequency of conflict between moral requirements and the interests of the agent. The development of the psychological structures that are implicated in moral motivation may in turn work to increase the rationality of moral conduct in two ways: by supplying the psychological conditions in which people can have reason to give moral requirements precedence over their own interests in cases of conflict, but also by providing people with strong motives to shape their interests so as to minimize such conflicts from the outset. Thus nurturing the psychological bases of moral motivation, in addition to fostering the acquisition of moral reasons, actually represents one of the ways in which social institutions can, indirectly, help to reduce the conflicts between morality and the interests of the agent. The other major way in which institutions can reduce such conflicts is by ensuring that they themselves satisfy the requirements of social justice. As we saw at the end of the previous chapter, individuals' attempts to shape their own interests so as to avoid conflict with morality are likelier to meet with success when there is a relatively wide range of activities in which they can engage without violating moral principles. The more unjust a society is, however, the greater the demands that morality makes of the individuals in it, and the narrower the range of morally acceptable pursuits that are likely to be open to a person. In a seriously unjust society, therefore, conflicts between moral requirements and the interests of the individual agent may be extremely difficult to avoid. That is, they may be difficult to avoid for those people who are not themselves the victims of serious injustice. The victims of injustice may find it easier to avoid such conflicts, since their strong interest in the elimination of injustice means that for them the demands of morality and the pursuit of their own advantage are likely to coincide. This is one of the few advantages of being a victim. On the whole, however, conflicts between morality and the interests of the agent will tend to be quite common in a seriously unjust society. In a fundamentally just society, by contrast, such conflicts may be much rarer.

Taken together, the foregoing reflections suggest that in a just and well-ordered society with strong traditions of civic responsibility and moral education, the occasions on which it would be rational for people to violate moral requirements would be minimized.[4] For in such a society conflicts between those requirements and the interests of the individual agent would be relatively infrequent. And when such conflicts did arise, the tendency of individuals to resolve them in favor of morality would be relatively strong, as would their reasons for doing so. In the ideal case it would never be rational in such a society for a person knowingly to do what morality prohibited. In other words, the claim of overridingness would be true, at least as applied to people in that society. Of course there is no reason whatsoever to suppose that this ideal could ever be fully realized, especially since the conditions that affect the rationality of moral conduct are not all subject to human control. Nevertheless, it is illuminating to think of it as a kind of limiting case. For when we do this, we can see that the overridingness of morality is in a sense a matter of degree, and that the maximization of overridingness may naturally be construed as a legitimate social goal. In other words, although it would be unreasonable to expect that there could be a society in which people always, without exception, had more reason to respect moral norms than to flout them, it may reasonably be thought both a practical social task and a feasible social goal to ensure that such circumstances obtain as frequently as possible.

It is no surprise to discover that living in a just society is a piece of good fortune. However, the preceding discussion highlights one of the less conspicuous reasons why this is so: namely, that in such a society it is much easier to shape one's interests so as to avoid conflicts with morality. Since the absence of conflict between the projects and commitments to which one is devoted and the demands

---

4. There are certain broad affinities between my remarks on this topic and Rawls's discussion of "the problem of congruence" in *A Theory of Justice* (Cambridge, Mass.: Harvard University Press, 1971).

of morality is greatly to be welcomed, it is obviously good fortune to find oneself living in a society where the chances of avoiding such conflict are relatively favorable. One of the many advantages of the just society is that it maximizes people's chances of securing harmony between their personal aims and the requirements of morality. This does not, of course, mean that it is impossible for an individual to achieve such harmony in an unjust society. We have already seen that those who are the victims of injustice may, precisely by virtue of their status as victims, find it relatively easy to do so. And it is certainly possible for people who are not victims to achieve such harmony: if, for example, the promotion of a more just society figures prominently among their own fundamental aims and aspirations. The claim is not that this is impossible, but rather that in a seriously unjust society the kinds of personal projects that are compatible with moral requirements are much more restricted, so that harmony between personal aims and moral demands is more difficult to achieve. By contrast, a person living in a just society will typically have a much wider array of pursuits and activities from which to choose, compatibly with living a morally unexceptionable life.

The point that I have been making might be summed up by saying that it is in one's interest to have one's interests be compatible with moral requirements, and that it is, therefore, in one's interest to live in a society where there is a good chance of securing such compatibility. This formulation may sound odd or even paradoxical, but the idea it expresses is perfectly clear and, in my view, correct. It does not mean that it is, on balance, always in one's interest to behave morally, but rather that it is generally in one's interest to avoid conflicts between one's (other) interests and morality's demands. In particular, one's overall interests are better served by avoiding such conflicts than by resolving them when they arise in favor of one's interests. This is partly because the experience of such conflict in itself has little to recommend it, and partly because there are obvious advantages to leading a morally acceptable life, even if they are not always sufficient to outweigh the advantages of defying morality in cases of conflict.

There is also another respect, closely related to the one I have been discussing, in which the person who lives in a just society is fortunate. In general, it is in one's interest to be comfortably integrated into the society in which one lives: not only to be a member in good standing of the society, with all the formal rights and privileges of membership, and not only to occupy a reasonably stable and rewarding social and economic role within the society, but also to find the society's culture and practices congenial, to experience one's own participation in them as natural, and to be regarded by others as a full-fledged fellow participant. Clearly there is much more to be said about what such integration consists in, and there are also obvious questions about what can count as a society for these purposes. In addition, generous allowance must be made for the numerous variations and idiosyncrasies that distinguish socially integrated lives from each other, for such integration is compatible with considerable diversity of personal style. In general, however, it is clear that integration of this kind is a benefit to the person who enjoys it. Moreover, there are close if complex relations between social integration and individual psychological integration, which it is also in one's interest to achieve. Although it is possible to attain either type of integration without the other, the processes by which the two are attained are closely linked, and in favorable circumstances the smooth operation of each process can enhance the smooth operation of the other.

Now, in any society that has widely shared moral norms, most people who succeed in achieving social and psychological integration will also have internalized the society's moral norms to at least some extent. This is an empirical claim, but not, I think, a terribly controversial one. It amounts only to the claim that a person who is both psychologically and socially well integrated is likely to have a moral sensibility that reflects to some significant degree the moral norms of his or her society. What makes this claim plausible is the fact that successful integration into a society is likely to require substantial compliance with its norms, together with the fact that this requirement is likely to be reflected in the firm expectations with which children at important stages of development are presented. Internalization of the relevant norms serves the interests of psychological integration by incorporating these inescapable but initially alien demands on one's motives and behavior into the self.[5] It serves

5. In the previous chapter I argued that adherence to moral norms enables one to integrate a respect for the worth of others with one's naturally disproportionate concern to lead a fulfilling life oneself. What I am claiming here is something different, namely, that in a society that has widely shared moral norms, it may be difficult to achieve a fully integrated personality of any kind without internalizing the society's norms to at least some extent.

the interests of social integration not only because it is an effective way of producing substantial compliance with society's norms, but also because it encourages a respect for the interests of others, and because it enables one to participate in an extraordinarily important aspect of the life of the culture: to share in reactions, values, and intuitions that together constitute one of the most important and distinctive dimensions of any human culture in which they make their presence felt.

The claim that people who are socially and psychologically well integrated will to some extent have internalized prevailing moral norms does not mean that such people cannot engage in moral criticism of their own society, only that when they do so their criticism is likely to be rooted in values or principles that have a high degree of social acceptance. They are less likely than people whose position in society is more marginal to experience the idea of a radical moral critique of the society as psychologically attractive, although there may of course be circumstances in which they are nevertheless driven to formulate or embrace such a critique.

The point of these remarks is not to dismiss radical criticism of society as a manifestation of poor psychological or social integration—far from it. It is rather to say that people have a strong interest in achieving forms of personal integration that tend to have the effect of encouraging moral conservatism, and that although this fact has its advantages, it also suggests that the reliability of the "commonsense" moral instincts shared by the members of a given society may depend to a significant extent on the justice or injustice of the society in question. In a seriously unjust society, well-intentioned people may have internalized moral attitudes that make the injustice of their institutions genuinely difficult for them to perceive, and all their instincts may testify to the society's moral soundness. By contrast, the people who find the injustices easier to perceive may be people who were already alienated from society in one way or another, and precisely because of their socially marginal status they may be dismissed by many well-intentioned and well-integrated people as mere cranks or gadflies. In an unjust society, however, the cranks and gadflies may be able to see some things more clearly than those who are better integrated.

This illustrates the way in which the ethical conversation of a culture like ours resembles a complex dance of moral judgment, psychological insight, and social analysis, requiring attention to motives as well as values, minds as well as morals, groups as well as individuals, causes as well as reasons, what is not said as well as what is said. It may also appear to support the view that people's moral intuitions lack any justificatory significance. That is not a conclusion that I myself would draw, however, since it is difficult for me to see how there could be any plausible conception of ethical justification that did not assign a substantial role of some kind to ethical beliefs and intuitions. On the other hand, the proper characterization of that role is obviously an exceedingly delicate matter, and the points that I have been making provide an additional reminder of this. That has not been my reason for making them, however. Instead, my purpose has been to call attention to something that is closely related to the previously discussed phenomenon of variability in the relationship between morality and the interests of the agent. Just as social institutions can influence the extent of conflict between individual moral requirements and the individual agent's interests, so too they can influence the degree of ease or difficulty with which it is possible to achieve both personal integration and unblinkered moral insight. For in an unjust society tension between these two aims is likely to grow as the amount of conflict between moral demands and the interests of agents increases. I do not mean that a person is likely to have to make a deliberate choice between moral insight and personal integration. Rather, my point is that, in an unjust society, patterns of personal development that are not themselves the objects of choice may tend to encourage the achievement of one aim, but only at the cost of making it more difficult to achieve the other. It is certainly true, and we have already seen, that unjust societies are more likely to present well-intentioned people with hard choices between the satisfaction of moral requirements and the advancement of cherished personal projects. In addition, however, what I am now suggesting is that such societies also tend to obscure the character of those very choices, and to encourage the development of moral sensibilities that can make it genuinely difficult for well-intentioned and well-integrated people accurately to perceive the moral conditions in which they live. Insofar as both personal integration and a truthful moral self-understanding contribute to the living of a good life, the difficulty in unjust societies of simultaneously achieving both adversely affects the quality of people's lives. In this respect, the promotion of social justice provides benefits, not only to those who have been the most conspicuous victims of injustice, but also to the members of society more generally. Again, this does not mean that conflicts can never arise between individual moral requirements and an individual agent's interests. But it does mean that there are certain important personal goods that are much more readily available in just societies; and among these are harmony between morality's demands and the aims of the self, and between the achievement of moral insight and the achievement of personal integration.

In this chapter I have tried to explain why, on my view, the relation between what an agent is morally required to do and what that agent has most reason to do may not be fixed or invariant, and may depend to a significant extent on the character of the prevailing social practices and institutions. In part, this is because the relation between moral requirements and the interests of the individual agent is influenced strongly, and in more than one way, by such practices and institutions. I have also argued that, since there are important personal goods whose availability depends in turn on the state of the relationship between moral demands and individual interests, the distribution of these goods is similarly affected by the structure and character of society. These points should serve to caution us against any excessively individualistic interpretation of the relations among reason, morality, and the interests of agents. In addition, they should serve to remind us of the extent to which the structures of moral decency, like many other precious but fragile resources, are social products. Human institutions can make decency more or less costly, and more or less difficult to achieve, and in these and other ways they can either discourage or nourish it. If, as I have been arguing in this book, morality is fundamentally a humane phenomenon, then not the least of the ways in which this is so is that it encourages decent human beings to contribute to the development of societies in which it may be easier for rational agents to be decent human beings.

INDEX

Adler, Jonathan, 110n
Agent-centered prerogative, 103, 105–6n
Agent-centered restrictions, 75
Agent-relative principles, 103–5, 107–8, 122n
Anscombe, G. E. M., 9n, 11n
Aristotle, 11, 14
Arlow, Jacob, 89n
Assessment, moral, 62, 113, 119; and deliberation, 21–23, 28–51; immunity to, 6, 17–25 (*see also* Pervasiveness; Scope of morality)
Attention change, 36–37
Authoritative considerations, 86–91, 94–95
Authoritative ideal, 89–90
Authoritative motivation, 86–96

Bad faith, 138
Blum, Lawrence, 15n, 110n
Brenner, Charles, 80n
Brink, David, 38n, 105–9
Broadie, Sarah, 118n
Brutality, 136

Categorical imperative(s), 64n, 84–87, 90
Chodorow, Nancy, 81n
Claim of overridingness (CO), 26–27, 52–61, 71–79, 95–97, 133–36, 140. *See also* Morality: overridingness of
Communitarian values, 14–16
Conflict, moral, 44–45
Conly, Sarah, 110n
Consequentialism, 108, 110, 121n. *See also* Utilitarianism
Cruelty, 136

Dancy, Jonathan, 47n
Davis, Nancy, 110n
Decision procedure, 39–51

Deliberation: and decision procedure, 39–51; and moral assessment, 21–23, 28–51; role of morality in, 5, 7, 8, 21–23, 28–51, 55, 64n, 128–29
Deontology, 20n, 42. *See also* Agent-centered restrictions; Agent-relative principles
Desires: broad sense of 'desire', 66, 92–94; and rationality of action, 53, 61, 73–74, 76 (*see also* Rationality: instrumental conception of); reasons not derived from, 90, 92, 96, 128–29, 134; reduction of values to, 137; role of, in moral motivation, 30–31n, 60–72, 78, 80–83, 85–96, 128; satisfied by moral conduct, 61n, 73; self-interested, 77 (*see also* Prudence; Rationality: prudential conception of; Self-interest); sexual and aggressive, 80–81; as source of reasons, 61, 73–74, 92, 134
Determinism, 63

Ego, 81, 84–85
Ego-ideal, 88–89
Egoism, naive psychological, 77–78
Emotions: importance of, for morality, 9, 14, 50; with moral presuppositions, 68–70, 95, 128–29, 138 (*see also* Resonance of morality)
Enlightenment values, 9–11, 16
Epistemological defiance, 15
Equal worth of persons, 16, 106–9, 122–26, 130
Error theory, 65, 67
Ethics of virtue, 11, 14
Eudaimonia, 118n
Externalism, ethical, 30n. *See also* Reasons for action: internal vs. external

Feinberg, Joel, 68n
Feminism, 14, 16

147